The Enigma of the Kerala Woman

Some Books from Social Science Press

India and China in the Colonial World (PB)
Edited by Madhavi Thampi

Telecommunications Industry in India: State, Business and Labour in a Global Economy (HB)
Dilip Subramanian

Reflections on Cambridge (HB)
Alan Macfarlane

Religious Division and Social Conflict: The Emergence of Hindu Nationalism in Rural India (PB)
Peggy Froerer

India's Economic Future: Education, Technology, Energy and Environment (HB)
Edited by Manmohan Agarwal

The Politics and Culture of Globalisation: India and Australia (HB)
Edited by Hans Löfgren and Prakash Sarangi

'Good Women do not Inherit Land': Politics of Land and Gender in India (HB)
Nitya Rao

New Mansions for Music: Performance, Pedagogy and Criticism (HB)
Lakshmi Subramanian

Writing History in the Soviet Union: Making the Past Work (HB)
Arup Banerji

Political Theologies: Public Religions in a Post-secular World (HB)
Edited by Hent de Vries and Lawrence E. Sullivan

Regulation, Institutions and the Law
Edited by Jaivir Singh

Globalization and the Millennium Development Goals: Negotiating the Challenge (HB)
Edited by Manmohan Agarwal and Amit Shovon Ray

Cultural History of Medieval India (PB)
Edited by Meenakshi Khanna

Cultural History of Modern India (PB)
Edited by Dilip M. Menon

Delhi: Ancient History (PB)
Edited by Upinder Singh

Unbecoming Modern: Colonialism, Modernity and Colonial Modernities (HB)
Edited by Saurabh Dube and Ishita Banerjee-Dube

Literature and Nationalist Ideology: Writing Histories of Modern Indian Languages (HB)
Edited by Hans Harder

The Sundarbans: Folk Deities, Monsters and Mortals (HB)
Sutapa Chatterjee Sarkar

The Many Worlds of Sarala Devi: A Diary
Sukhendu Ray
&
The Tagores and Sartorial Styles (HB)
Malavika Karlekar

After the Iraq War: The Future of the UN and International Law (HB)
Edited by Bernhard Vogel, Rudolf dolzer and Matthias Herdegen

Social and Economic Profile of India (HB)
(In full colour)
Peeyush Bajpai, Laveesh Bhandari and Aali Sinha

Everyday Politics of Labour: Working Lives in India's Informal Economy (HB)
Geert De Neve

Viramma: Life of a Dalit (PB)
Viramma, Josiane Racine and Jean-Luc Racine

Lived Islam in South Asia: Adaptation, Accommodation and Conflict (HB)
Edited by Imtiaz Ahmad and Helmut Reifeld

Reforming India's Social Sector: Poverty, Nutrition, Health and Education (HB)
Edited by K. Seeta Prabhu and R. Sudarshan

Human Security in South Asia: Energy, Gender, Migration, and Globalisation (HB)
Edited by P.R. Chari and Sonika Gupta

Religion and Personal Law in Secular India: A Call to Judgment (HB)
Edited by Gerald James Larson

Trade, Finance and Investment in South Asia (HB)
Edited by T.N. Srinivasan

Forthcoming

Unruly Hills: Nature and Nation in India's Northeast
Bengt G. Karlsson

The Enigma of the Kerala Woman

A Failed Promise of Literacy

Edited by
Swapna Mukhopadhyay

SOCIAL SCIENCE PRESS

Published by
Esha Béteille
Social Science Press
69 Jor Bagh, New Delhi 110 003

First published in 2007
Paperback edition 2011

ISBN 978-81-87358-44-2

Set in Giovanni Book
Typeset by Eleven Arts, Delhi 110 035
Printed by De-Unique, Delhi 110 018

Contents

LIST OF TABLES

LIST OF FIGURES

Preface to the Paperback Edition

Writing the Preface to a new edition of a book is always a pleasure. Especially so if it is nowhere near a polished piece of work, with all the dots and commas in place and all the questions raised in it neatly answered. It is good to know that even so, the first edition is sold out: that the ideas contained in the book have found an audience.

That literacy is an essential ingredient in women's empowerment is a proposition that nobody would contest.' However, what is sometimes forgotten is that the reverse is not necessarily true. The book is a testimony to this phenomenon. The enigma of the Kerala woman consists in the fact that in spite of her high literacy, she carries the burden of socially ordained gender discrimination round her neck, like most other seemingly less endowed, and less capable of her sisters around the country. Why does this happen?

Although it took a long time and years of multi-disciplinary research with scholars cutting across many disciplines to zero in on the truth, the answer is actually quite simple. After all, literacy is only an instrument of empowerment. Its potency lies in how it is used. If used pro-actively, it opens up the mind, it enables the person to question and analyse received wisdom. Only then does it become an ennobling power of the mind, and a formidable force to reckon with. Only then can it challenge deep seated prejudices and work towards altering mind sets. If instead, literacy is used as an instrument to reinforce pre-existing discriminatory ideas and practices, it will sabotage rather than initiate that process of change. An 'indicator', however good, can never be a perfect substitute of what it seeks to indicate. The material contained in the book—research papers, case studies, visuals—bears testimony to the fallacy of that equation.

Perhaps the true value of the book, if any, lies not so much in the answer, but the laborious process through which it was reached. It was indeed a truly multi-disciplinary endeavour. The research design was new and so were many of the ingredients that went into it. Perhaps for the first time, Mental Health has been integrated in quantitative gender analysis in a manner as has been done here. Drawing upon the literature on threat of violence as a concept in sociological studies, and the concept of 'credible threat' in the Theory of Games in economics, it has been possible to use psychological measures of gender related stress and anxiety for analysing the phenomenon of Violence Against Women (VAW). In our view, this is a far more useful and sensible way of handling the phenomenon in quantitative analysis than for instance, measuring it by the number of times a wife gets beaten up, which has been the prevailing practice until now.

What the book does is to sound an alarm bell against mindless substitution of 'indicators' for the phenomenon they are supposed to indicate. Informed policy decisions for eradicating social discrimination, be it against women or against backward castes, need to be based not simply on heedless recording of 'indicators', however many, but on deep rooted understanding of the phenomena and their manifestations in specific contexts.

There are many ideas and propositions in the book that have been suggested but not fully worked out. If researchers from diverse disciplines pick up those loose threads and carry forward the investigation, we will consider our labour to be amply rewarded.

Swapna Mukhopadhyay
Gurgaon, India
1 August 2010

Preface and Acknowledgements

This book took a long time in coming. For somebody entrusted with the job of designing and directing an inter-country research programme on gender, the contradictory signals of women's empowerment from Kerala had stuck out like a sore thumb. The search for a convincing understanding of the curious case of the Kerala woman had started fairly early in the Gender Network research agenda. But not until recently did things seem to fall in place. The search process has taken a long time. The introductory chapter contains the history of this search in some detail.

It is a pleasure to acknowledge the many individuals and organizations that have helped me in putting this book together. My first debt of gratitude is to the authors of the papers included in this volume and all the others who have been part of the Kerala team of researchers over the years. This includes researchers from the Centre for Development Studies (CDS) in Thiruvananthapuram who have collaborated with us in earlier phases of the Gender Network; the team of dedicated doctors under the stewardship of Dr E. Mohamed who were instrumental in carrying out the field survey on mental health in Kerala; several of my younger colleagues who were associated with the work at various stages and in various capacities at the Institute of Social Studies Trust (ISST) where the Gender Network project was stationed, and especially Rajib Nandi who was a boon to have as a colleague at ISST. I will continue to miss Professor Ravi Kapur, and his brilliant presence and sense of humour. He provided me with the inputs on mental health, which turned out to be so crucial for this research. His able student and co-author, Shobna Sonpar, became an integral part of the project at a crucial stage of its development. J. Devika, the feminist historian from CDS, has enlightened me in many ways, and has been a pleasure to know and work with. My special thanks to her.

A debt of gratitude must go to the International Development Research Centre (IDRC) of Canada and the various programme officers who have from time to time been in charge of the Gender Network Project in that organization. They gave me the space and the latitude to follow the leads in designing the research agenda on Kerala, often in a manner, which could not be foreseen at the time of writing the project proposals. Our debt to the agency is considerable also because it has financially supported this research for several years at the ISST, during my tenure at that organization as the Director, and having continued to do so until such time that the project came to an end.

Finally I owe a huge debt to Social Science Press (SSP), for the meticulous professionalism that it has brought to this publication. It has been a great pleasure working with Esha. My sincere thanks go to Meenakshi Chawla who has worked on the script ceaselessly with care and patience. Thanks are also due to Meera Juneja who prepared an exhaustive index, all of which we have not been able to carry here, in a very short span of time.

To my husband Badal, I will be eternally grateful for smilingly suffering a volatile wife through the ups and down of this work.

Swapna Mukhopadhyay
March 2007

List of Contributors

Swapna Mukhopadhyay
Former Professor of Economics at the Institute of Economic Growth and former Director at the Institute of Social Studies Trust, New Delhi. She is currently involved as an advisor in some international development projects and occasionally teaches courses in Economics at various universities in the city.

She also plays the violin and teaches Western classical music at the Delhi School of Music.

S. Irudaya Rajan
Chair Professor of the Research Unit on International Migration at the Centre for Development Studies, Thiruvananthapuram, Kerala.

Sreerupa
Research scholar at the Centre for Development Studies, Thiruvananthapuram, Kerala.

Jayanti Basu
Psychoanalyst and a Rehabilitation Psychologist. She is Head of the Department of Applied Psychology, Calcutta University.

J. Devika
A historian and research associate at the Centre for Development Studies, Thiruvananthapuram, Kerala. She has published in English and Malayalam, on social history and the evolution of gender in Kerala.

Avanti Mukherjee
Research scholar in the Centre for Economic Studies and Planning, Jawaharlal Nehru University, New Delhi.

Jipson Sikhera
Photo journalist based in Cochin, Kerala.

SECTION 1

chapter one

Understanding the Enigma of Women's Status in Kerala

Does High Literacy Necessarily Translate into High Status?

Swapna Mukhopadhyay

NATURE OF THE 'ENIGMA'

The state of Kerala, a state of thirty odd million people in the southern tip of India, has been hailed as the epitome of women's development in a country that does not fare too well in terms of UNDP's gender development indicator.[1] Unlike many other states in this country of billion plus people, literacy levels are high among women as well as men in Kerala, and the differences between the two are relatively low, thereby contributing to a high level of recorded GDI in the state. Health indicators in the state are equally impressive, with high levels of life expectancy for women and men, and indeed a fairly strong positive tilt towards women, which is the case in all developed countries and—given the greater biological vulnerability of the male of the species as compared to the female—is

This introductory chapter provides a background to the research on the issue of gender in Kerala which was carried out under the auspices of the MIMAP-Gender Network, a multi-country thematic project sponsored by the International Development Research Centre (IDRC) of Canada at the Institute of Social Studies Trust (ISST), New Delhi India. The Gender Network Project was conceived and coordinated by the author during her tenure as the Director of ISST and Project Director of the Gender Network Project.

[1]According to the 2005 Human Development Report of UNDP, in the year 2003, India ranked 98 in a group of 140 countries with a GDI of 0.586, a few notches above Bangladesh (rank 105, GDI 0.514) Nepal (rank 106, GDI 0.511), and Pakistan (rank 107, GDI 0.508), but way below China (rank 64, GDI 0.754) or Sri Lanka (rank 66, GDI 0.747)

Table 1.1 Gender Differences in Selected Human Development Indicators in Kerala and a few other Indian States

State	*Literacy (Census 2001)*		*Life Expectancy at birth (1998–2002)*		*HDI (2001)*
	Male	*Female*	*Male*	*Female*	*Total*
Kerala	**94.20**	**87.86**	**70.8**	**75.9**	**0.638 (1)**
Bihar	71.93	56.03	61.4	59.5	0.367 (15)
Madhya Pradesh	76.80	50.28	57.0	56.7	0.394 (12)
Uttar Pradesh	84.01	60.26	59.4	58.5	0.388 (13)
Maharastra	86.27	67.51	65.0	67.0	0.523 (4)
Punjab	75.63	63.55	67.4	69.5	0.537 (2)
All India	**75.96**	**54.25**	**61.6**	**63.3**	**0.472**

Source: Economic Survey 2005–2006, Government of India
Note: Figures within brackets in the last column are ranks among the major states of India

what it should be in all relatively gender neutral societies. Even those health indicators that do not enter directly into the GDI calculations, such as maternal mortality rates, for instance, are pretty good in Kerala, the estimates being significantly lower than those in many other Indian states. It is little wonder that experts have cited the instance of Kerala as one that can and should be emulated to ensure high levels of gender development and consequently a high status for women.[2]

The MIMAP-Gender Network Research Project was launched with the purpose of investigating the gender differentiated 'micro impact of macro adjustment policies' in developing countries—MIMAP being the acronym for the phrase. In designing the research for this project, it was felt that restricting oneself solely to the measurable economic dimensions of the impact would be an inadequate way of handling the problem. Much of the 'work' routinely done by women is either not deemed to be 'economically productive', or is not measured because of inadequacy of data. Besides, since 'gender' is after all, a social construct, any investigation on the gender-differentiated effects of economic policy changes must logically look at the holistic picture so as to capture the multi-dimensional manifestations of such impact.

Although initially investigation into the Kerala case was not part of the project design, somewhere during the first phase of the Gender Network Project, a number of contradictory signals from the state

[2]A.K.Sen (2000); Dreze and Sen (1995).

made it imperative that one looked into the Kerala story in some detail. Despite the obvious achievements of the state in terms of the standard indicators of gender development, a little exploration outside these indicators brought up more questions than could be answered. One discovered that Kerala has one of the highest rates of recorded crimes against women, and among the highest incidence of domestic violence. Even if one allowed for considerable reporting bias, the figures were far too high for comfort in a state that boasts of a high status for women. There is growing evidence of female foeticide in Kerala, which suggests that, like in many other places in India, female babies are less valued than their male counterparts in Malayalee society. And if anything, things have been getting worse over the years. Kerala has been one state where historically, sex ratios have not been adverse against women. But things are changing. Infant sex ratio in every single district in Kerala had declined between the Census years 1981 and 1991, something that one discovered in the course of mapping age-wise sex ratios across all districts of India in the early stages of Gender Network research. It is this unexpected discovery that had initially set the alarm bells ringing. Although the trend has been halted in some of the districts in the later decade, this was too unnatural and too disturbing a piece of evidence to set aside without further probing.

Soon one became conscious of warning signals from other areas as well. In spite of high female literacy, as per the data provided by the quinquennial surveys carried out by the National Sample Survey Organization (NSSO), the state has among the lowest female labour force participation rates. Detailed interviews with women from varied socio-economic backgrounds under different contexts revealed that, contrary to popular belief, women do not enjoy the kind of 'freedom' that one would expect them to have given the high levels of human or gender development. The Gender Network research agenda slowly acquired a new item, namely unravelling the puzzle of the Kerala woman. We needed to understand how, such high levels of standard (or 'conventional') gender development indicators could co-exist with signals of women's powerlessness.

THE STORY IN BRIEF

The story begins with the 'discovery' that although, information was already available from different sources that questioned the dominant understanding of women enjoying a non-discriminatory and high social standing in Kerala, it did not shape popular knowledge and understanding of the issue. Such popular understanding has, after all, been supported by a range of sociological and historical explanations. Kerala has had a long history of social reforms, touching just about every community in the state. Almost all reformers have emphasized the vital role that women can, and should play in the reforms process. The high status traditionally enjoyed by women in matrilineal systems, of which Kerala could boast a few, the history of early spread of female education in the state through the agency of benevolent rulers as well as Christian missionaries, the seemingly proactive role played by the state government in the post-independence years in terms of early inception of family planning, the long history of the Left movement which had pushed the interests of the economically disadvantaged sections of the population, were some of the elements of the set of explanations that have been invoked to cement the popular understanding. The major indicators of women's development, such as literacy levels and health indicators, were far ahead of the rest of the states in India, and the dominant understanding about the status of women far too well entrenched for the contrary information, such as falling infant sex ratios or soaring dowry rates in the state in recent times, to make any dent in popular perception. High rates of crimes against women could be ignored by ascribing it to reporting bias due to high literacy levels. Low levels of female labour force participation could be explained away by invoking self-selection. Evidence contrary to prevalent notions of gender development coming out of detailed case studies could be ignored as aberrations.

Curiosity drove us to Kerala to understand the nature of the ground reality regarding women's status in the state.

A number of studies were conducted under the Gender Network Project during the period 1999 to 2006 to find out what, if anything was wrong with the 'status of women' in Kerala. The first of these was designed to review the history of social and legal reforms in the state with a focus on women's position in society (Eapen and Kodoth 2001). This study was supplemented by a number of intensive case studies of women cutting across various socio-economic divides. The second was a survey of mental health of women and men in Kerala, referred to in this volume, as the Kerala Mental Health Survey (KMHS), which was carried out on a representative sample of one thousand households covering over five thousand men and women from all fourteen districts of the state (E. Mohamed et al. 2002). The third study was a gender impact evaluation study of the Akshaya Project, a high profile and seemingly gender neutral state government project in the Information Technology sector (Mukhopadhyay and Nandi 2006). The three papers written specifically for these volumes during the third phase of the project bring up the rear.

LIMITATIONS OF CONVENTIONAL INDICATORS OF 'WOMEN'S STATUS'

The claims about the high levels of gender development in Kerala have been based, primarily, on high levels of recorded gender development indicators such as female literacy and life expectancy levels, and women's earnings in the labour market relative to that of men as expounded by UNDP. One has to take cognizance of the fact that a note of caution was indeed sounded in the original UNDP document, with a plea to take these figures with a degree of caution and to desist from reading too much into them. Subsequent years however, witnessed a virtual flood of research in gender studies with the collection and analysis of data on conventional 'gender development' indicators, in a range of social, economic, demographic and political arenas, over time and across space.[3]

This has been a useful development in so far as gender disaggregated information has become more easily accessible for ready reference. Most of these indicators may well be good indices of gender development in most situations. However, as with all statistical information, especially when one is dealing with something as nebulous as the 'status of women', one needs to be cautious in interpreting the body of data. Sometimes two different indicators of gender development may pull in different directions, making the job of construction of linear indices next to impossible.[4] Even in isolation, depending on the context, each one of these indicators may turn out to be limited in scope, for many of these are only instrumental indicators of women's status. They can indicate, at best, necessary, but not sufficient conditions for women's empowerment.

Take, for instance, the three basic indicators that constitute the gender development index promoted by UNDP i.e., gender differences in literacy, life expectancy and wage earnings. High levels of literacy

[3]Some of the earliest set of papers in India in this genre were published in the Special Issue on Gender in the *Economic and Political Weekly*, Vol. 31, No. 43, 1996; many others followed in subsequent years.

[4]Female literacy and labour force participation of women for instance, may pull in different directions in situations influenced by the process of 'Sanskritization'. Cf. M.N. Srinivas (1952). Also, Mukhopadhyay (1999).

open up the world of written communication to the individual, sharpening one's mental abilities and unleashing the potential for individual growth. It is no wonder that literacy has been accorded a prominent place in the literature on human and gender development. How that heightened potential is utilized for personal growth, however, is the defining issue. This will vary from one situation to another, and from one person to the next, depending on objective conditions and personal parameters and preferences. A literate woman may decide, or indeed be persuaded to decide, to use this new instrument to internalize the message of women's subordination to men all through her life, simply by virtue of being born a woman. Adherence to the dictum from Hindu scriptural writings in *Manusmriti*, which ordains that a woman be subordinate to her father in childhood, her husband in adulthood and her son in her old age, is unlikely to be an empowering message as far as the issue of women's status is concerned.[5] Similarly, better longevity may simply translate into long years of lonely and debilitating widowhood.[6] Participation in the labour market may bring in earnings for the woman, but not necessarily ensure her control over those earnings.

Therefore, in tracking human development and indeed gender development, which is a more complicated phenomenon since it involves not simply individuals, but relationships between them in an essential way, it is vitally important that one is conscious of situations where the instruments could have failed to successfully address the reality they are implicitly believed to have addressed. It is necessary, therefore, to go beyond a mechanical reading of the messages contained in these conventional 'gender indicators', to a search for triangulation of the evidence from other sources.

In this search for the portrayal of reality, the 'outliers' play a very important role. If all essential dimensions of gender bias were identified, and aligned together, any one of them could be a good indicator of the real picture. Only when some essential dimensions are missing, *and* when things tend to pull in different directions, one needs to investigate further. Qualitative evidence on certain dimensions of women's lives in Kerala, such as the evidence on gender violence and crimes against women, has been vitally important in Gender Network research in Kerala. It has impelled supplementary

[5]Cf. *'The Laws of Manu'*. Translation of 'Manu-Smriti' from Sanskrit by Wendy Doniger (1992).

[6]Cf. paper by Rajan and Sreerupa in this volume.

qualitative and quantitative research into related issues, and subsequently into supplementary 'indicators' that can capture some of these essentially qualitative dimensions of gender relations. Since gender relations are first and foremost, about the relative power balance between the sexes, an inquiry on gender has prompted one to look for manifestations of gender-based power relationships that are more direct and immediate in society and the community that one is interested in. No other indicator of women's powerlessness is as telling and as immediate as violence against women.

VIOLENCE AGAINST WOMEN IN KERALA

Violence, or its Credible Threat as the Key Indicator of Powerlessness

The first step in addressing the 'enigma' of the Kerala Woman has been to recognize that there is clear, incontrovertible evidence of extensive violence against women (VAW) in Kerala society. This was garnered from the review of a number of recent studies and sample surveys on VAW, as well as several case studies and individual interviews that were conducted by other researchers and by the Gender Network research team under various projects.[7] It was felt that whatever the extent of the 'recording bias', even if a fraction of the evidence was true, it raises serious questions about the supposed high status of women in the state, for there is no better indicator of the powerlessness of an individual or a group of people in a society or community than evidence of systemic violence, or a credible threat of such violence.

It needs to be emphasized here that it is not just evidence on actual perpetrated violence that one should be looking at. Even if there is a credible threat of such violence that is endemic to the society, a threat that may not even be carried out in a majority of cases, but which keeps women 'in place', and which acts as a powerful deterrent dissuading women from crossing the socially ordained boundaries of 'good womanhood', it is evidence that should tell us that something is not quite right with women's status. This is true not just where women are concerned. The threat could exist for any identified group of people in a community—be it dalits, ethnic groups or religious minorities. A community that tacitly tolerates systemic violence against them, or covertly supports a credible threat of such violence, cannot at the same time boast of ascribing a high status to those at

[7]UNIFEM (2000), ICRW (2000), Mukherji, Rastogi and Krishnaji (2001), CWDS (2002), ISST (2000), Saravanan (2001), Mukhopadhyay and Nandi (2006).

the receiving end. Extensive interviews with Kerala women from varied backgrounds using a range of qualitative methods such as case studies, focus group discussions and detailed life histories over the course of the research convinced us that not everything is right for women in 'God's Own Country'.[8]

Even at the very beginning of the Gender Network Project, before the Kerala studies were initiated, one had been aware of the possibility that, for a variety of reasons, high levels of 'conventional' gender development indicators such as those that are included in the GDI, may not necessarily translate into high 'status' of women in a particular context, however defined. In order to get a fuller understanding of the elusive phenomenon of status, one has also to look into other indicators, which for want of a better term, we called 'non-conventional' indicators of gender development,—violence and its credible threat being the most important component of the latter set.[9]

'Measuring' Violence

The next issue is to figure out how best to 'measure' this phenomenon. This was deemed necessary so that violence, and its credible threat, could be mapped against other, more conventional indicators of 'status' to bring possible contradictions into clearer focus. It was felt that it is best if it could be done without having to go after the sordid task of counting how many times a woman gets beaten up, by whom and under what circumstances, or what are the tangible forms of mental torture she is subjected to: questions which are barely ever answered truthfully in standard household surveys. Instead, it was felt, that one could take an altogether different course. One could argue that violence and a credible threat of such violence, in overt or in muted forms in one's daily life, is likely to raise the levels of stress and anxiety in women, *other things remaining the same*. If this argument has some validity, then one could induct available instruments of applied psychology to measure levels of stress and anxiety, and use these indicators as surrogates, so to speak. These psychometric variables could then be used in conjunction with other standard socio-economic variables in order to explore a range of issues using available multivariate quantitative techniques.

[8]The expression used by the State Government of Kerala to promote tourism in the state.

[9]See Mukhopadhyay (1998) and Mukhopadhyay (2003) for a fuller exposition.

This course has some advantages and some disadvantages. The advantages are that there are well established measures of stress and anxiety, and also of mental well-being, which are believed to be reasonably 'culture free' and which have been tested and widely used by applied psychologists in a large number of countries. The other advantage is of course that these indicators being quantitative, or more accurately, categorical in nature, can be used in conjunction with standard socio-economic variables from household surveys in multivariate analysis.

In addition, the use of these mental health indicators within a broader framework of socio economic household surveys has the potential of bringing together two different strains of research, and researchers, who have been investigating issues of gender discrimination on a common platform; i.e., sociologists, social anthropologists and some feminist scholars on the one hand who have been primarily using qualitative methods, and applied econometricians and others of similar persuasion who have been using various gender development indicators within quantitative frameworks. During the course of conducting research under some other modules of the Gender Network research, these instruments of mental health were included in household surveys that were being carried out in several countries of South and South East Asia.[10] One was pleasantly surprised at the ease with which these survey instruments could be administered in the field.

The major disadvantage in moving from VAW to mental health in the present context, is that the jump may appear to be far too abrupt. There can indeed, be a host of factors other than gender-related ones that can, and do cause mental stress. However, one can try to correct this, even if partially, by various methods. Through triangulation by qualitative methods, such as properly designed case studies or FDGs, one can try to assess the strength of the linkages between gender violence and mental stress of women under various situations. Efforts to apply such techniques have been made in individual country studies

[10]Unpublished versions of the reports of various Gender Network studies carried out in the first two phases of the research have been compiled in nine volumes which are available at the ISST Library. See the section titled 'Additional References' at the end of this paper for a full listing. Mental health instruments were included in surveys of 'Gender and Poverty' in six countries, surveys of worker households in Export Processing Zones (EPZ) and Export Oriented Units (EOU) in four countries and surveys of retrenched worker households in two. These are contained in volumes IV, VII and VIII respectively.

but not reported here. The second way could be through multiple regression analysis where efforts can be made to net out the influence of other factors by including them, to the extent possible, as explanatory variables in the model. The third is to go one step further and try to establish the linkages of the two by directly inducting into the multivariate analysis some kind of a 'gender ideology index' as an additional explanatory variable. This approach has been tried out using the Kerala Mental Health Survey (KMHS) data in a paper that has been included in this volume.[11]

Understanding Routine Violence against Women

Recent research carried out by organizations and individual researchers suggests that routine violence against women is high in Kerala.[12] The state also has the dubious distinction of having the highest recorded rate of crimes against women.[13] Even after correcting for reporting bias that is sometimes presumed to be lower in Kerala than the national average because of high literacy rates in the state, the figures are far too high for comfort, especially for a state that has been hailed as the epitome of gender development.

What propels such widespread violence against women in a state where women are so highly literate? Many scholars have dwelt upon the phenomenon of violence, its nature and its raison d'etre. Violence in our troubled time has invoked all kinds of concerns and explanations, from class conflicts expounded under the Marxist philosophy, to political ramifications of mass psychology,[14] to the consolidation of dominant identities through everyday quotidian acts.[15]

While the latter may not be a good characterization for understanding political violence in the ordinary sense of the term, perhaps it comes closest to characterizing power relationships spawned by the politics of gender, hence understanding the routine violence perpetrated against women. This is what seems to be behind the gender violence that cuts across social boundaries. The identity ingrained in

[11]Cf. Mukhopadhyay, Basu and Rajan in this volume.

[12]The ICRW study, for instance, puts Kerala as the state with the highest incidence of domestic violence among some of the major states in India where the survey was carried out.

[13]Cf. Mukherjee, Rastogi and Krishnaji.

[14]The classic reference on this is Hannah Arendt.

[15]For a recent exposition on this line of thought, see *Routine Violence: Nations, Fragments, Histories* by Gyanendra Pandey, Stanford University Press, 2006.

the Indian male is that he is superior to the woman. This understanding may remain unspoken, though it has commonly understood ramifications within different social contexts. Within the marital relationship, for instance, the husband has a right to the body and the mind of the woman he is married to. Domestic violence is different from other forms of violence against women, in that, it is bred and nurtured on a one-to-one basis, within the four walls of the home, and perpetrated by individuals on whom depends the very identity of the woman. The same logic of male identity is seen to be carried over to the arena outside the domestic sphere, and can, in many cases, explain instances of 'crimes against women' in 'normal' times, and forms an integral part of the set of factors that has been invoked to explain mass violence against women in troubled times like those of conflict and communal disturbance.

For a largely literate segment of the population like Kerala women, the question that needs to be answered is why women tolerate routine domestic violence and the pervasive threat of 'crimes against women' outside the home. As some of the case studies in this volume suggest, this could be a result of the perceived absence of any fallback option outside marriage, however abusive it may be and the fear of perceived transgression from the prescribed societal norms that a woman must be married. To that extent, it may be a time-tested survival strategy for the woman, honed and sculpted by generations of experience and propelled by the credible threat of a world outside, which could be far worse than an abusive marriage.

To a certain extent, however, it could also be the result of the internalization of the patriarchal order that invests in the man of the household, not merely an unquestioned right over the body of the woman, but also the right to disciplinary action at his will, supposedly propelled by perceived deviations from patriarchal norms widely subscribed to by the community. It is important to note that the wide acceptance of male superiority in the community, however covert, is a necessary condition for the persistence of widespread domestic abuse.

Violence against Women, Mental Health and Gender Ideology

During the survey on mental health in Kerala, a set of questions was administered to all adults in the sample to assess the extent to which they subscribe to the traditional gender ideology that puts the male above the female in the social hierarchy. A Gender Ideology Index was constructed using a randomly selected sample of 200 households from the set of 1000 surveyed in the KMHS. This index was then used as an explanatory variable along with other socio-economic indicators on the respondents from the remaining 800 households. There were two mental health indicators on which data were collected during the survey; these are GHQ (General Health Questionnaire) and SUBI (Subjective Well Being Indicator). Two versions of both these mental health indicators were used in the various versions of the equations. One is based on the individual scores in continuous form, and the second is the binary form of the indices which are used in applied psychology to identify potential problem cases.

Analysing these measures of mental health in conjunction with other socio-economic indices and mapping these against an index of gender ideology has helped in unearthing the complex interlinkages of these variables. In the absence of any established theory relating these variables, the basic model used is that of a simple single equation variety. The results of the multiple regression analysis reported in the paper by Mukhopadhyay, Basu and Rajan referred to above, demonstrate fairly stable statistical associations between a patriarchal gender ideology and higher levels of mental stress and anxiety. This association turns out to be stable across alternative variable as well as alternative model specifications. What comes out strongly from the data is that the level of mental distress is fairly high in Kerala for both men and women, and also that it is consistently higher for women as compared to men. The women in our sample also appear to subscribe to patriarchal ideology to a greater extent than the men. What is most interesting is the result that subscribing to a patriarchal gender ideology is a much more potent, or statistically significant explanation for mental stress in women than it is in men.

USING 'NON-CONVENTIONAL' INDICATORS TO UNDERSTAND THE NATURE OF THE PUZZLE

These results strengthen our earlier hypothesis that women in Kerala may be suffering from high levels of stress and anxiety, and some of that stress could be linked to gender related factors. However, while the introduction of the mental health dimension does help us to probe deeper into the phenomenon of women's well being, it does not quite answer the question we started off with, in the first place. Namely, it does not tell us why the average Kerala woman continues to cling to patriarchal values despite suffering from high stress levels, when she has the potential for breaking free by virtue of her education. Our results seem to offer only a partial answer to that puzzle, i.e. perhaps women tolerate such gender-related stress because they subscribe to norms of patriarchy which put women squarely below men in social hierarchies, so that the message of subordination to the male, along with all it entails, including gender violence, may have been internalized to a significant extent in the women's psyche.

The question can now be asked in a different form: What are the factors that could have been behind such internalization? Why do Kerala women, highly educated as they are, subscribe to an ideology that invests women with an inferior status?

To explore this enigma, we have had to go back to qualitative methods once again: case studies, life histories and history of social movements in Kerala. There could be two interrelated answers to this issue. An informed reading of the history of social reforms in the state from a feminist perspective suggests that while all social reformers have emphasized the importance of female literacy, the proposed 'emancipation' of women has invariably been looked upon as an instrument that is to be used for the benefit of the family and society, not for the benefit of the woman as an individual in her own right. Literacy may even have been an instrument facilitating the process of internalization of that message. The message has clearly gone very deep in Kerala society, for in terms of gender related issues in public life, Malayalee society continues to be very conservative.

A second reason could be a steady erosion of fallback options for women over time. A study of the history of legal reforms in the state shows how the state has acted as an agency for facilitating the gradual erosion of property rights and increasing economic vulnerability of women in Kerala. The passivity of the average woman in gender related matters could be the manifestation of a deeply entrenched survival strategy that comes out of an understanding that all things told, staying on in an abusive marriage may be a far better option than walking out of it.

'CONVENTIONAL' AND 'NON-CONVENTIONAL' INDICATORS

So here is a situation where high female literacy goes hand in hand with passive submission to male domination. One would think that true internalization of traditional norms of patriarchy by the average person in Kerala, i.e., when both the men and the women in a household truly shared the same patriarchal values would, *ceteris paribus*, lead to lower evidence of gender-based dissonance within the household than otherwise. By the same token, if women of the household start questioning norms of patriarchal subordination in contradiction to the values held by men, one would expect that, other things remaining the same, instances of domestic dissonance and strife would increase. In another study, in a survey of two thousand households in the states of Uttar Pradesh and Karnataka, men and women from the same households in Uttar Pradesh (U.P.) were found to share the same values about gender relations.[16] There was much less evidence of domestic strife and violence within the households in the U.P. sample as compared to a similar study from Karnataka, where men and women had different views on gender. The women in U.P. were much less educated than the Karnataka women and had far less exposure to the outside world. In other words, in terms of standard indicators of women's status, Karnataka was far ahead of U.P. Yet evidence of domestic strife and violence against women was much more rampant in the Karnataka sample as compared to the one from U.P.

The U.P. situation was, therefore, a combination of relatively poor levels of 'conventional' gender development indicators and relatively good 'non-conventional' gender development (GD) indicators in so far as reported levels of domestic violence go. The Karnataka sample instead, combined relatively better conventional GD indicators with relatively worse recorded levels of non-conventional indicators.[17] One could try to explain why these combinations may have arisen in the two cases. In case of U.P., it is possibly the outcome of shared values of male dominance cemented by a process of socialization unchallenged by competing norms brought in by external exposure through literacy or paid work. In case of Karnataka where the women were somewhat more literate and engaged in work outside the home in much larger numbers than their U.P. counterparts, the absence of adherence to shared gender norms brought about by external exposure would have unsettled the traditional balance of power, which was evident in terms of high rates of reported marital discord.[18]

The Kerala case does not seem to fall into either of these categories. Here, high incidence of domestic violence and crimes against women coexist with high female literacy levels, higher than is the case in Karnataka. However, unlike in Karnataka, reporting of marital discord was much lower in the Kerala sample. How does one explain this phenomenon? As mentioned earlier, this could be due to a couple

[16]Cf. Mukhopadhyay and Savithri, 1998.

[17]For an exposition on the problems of handling contradictory messages indicated by the two categories of indicators, see Mukhopadhay (2003).

[18]See Mukhopadhyay and Savitri 1998.

of interrelated factors. It could be a calculated survival strategy that prevents the average woman in Kerala from protesting against the abuse, or a credible threat of such abuse if she deviates from the prescribed societal norms. Or it could be that in the perception of women, the fallback options are worse than the abuse. Yet unlike the U.P. woman, who is illiterate and has virtually no exposure to the world of paid work, the Kerala woman can, in principle, be economically independent. The society does not frown on women working for pay in Kerala!

There could be a third hypothesis that may also explain this phenomenon of resigned acceptance of the norms of male dominance. The paper on mental health included in this volume suggests that Kerala women strongly favour orthodox gender ideology, even more than Kerala men. It is possible to hypothesize then, that the potential accorded to women by high literacy may have been utilized, not so much in questioning norms of male superiority, but in internalizing the message and consolidating it in their lives. The *Manusmriti* factor may actually have played a role in cementing these views.

Unlike in U.P. or Karnataka, the survey in Kerala drew a blank on direct questions on domestic violence. Most women refused to answer these questions. This is understandable, because compared to the relatively unlettered rural women in the U.P. who may accept minor incidences of violence as routine, or those in the Karnataka sample who may not have been 'Sanskritized' enough to question them, the literate woman sampled in the Mental Health Survey in Kerala would be less willing to openly confess to violence within her home, or a threat to such violence if she goes against societal norms.[19]

If indeed this is so, could one then perhaps argue, that this is the price that Kerala woman pays for her high literacy levels? That the potential of logic and reasoning that she is invested with by dint of her education, may be instrumental in creating the high level of mental stress, which the illiterate woman from the U.P. study is spared from.

Even if it were indeed the case, nobody in her right mind would argue that women in Kerala would be better off if they were more like their U.P. counterparts, i.e. if they were not literate. The evidence

[19]It is interesting to note that a similar situation also obtains in Sri Lanka where female literacy rates are high but women are routinely subjected to actual and credible threats of violence and indignities such as pre-marital virginity tests. Cf. Wanasundera and other CENWOR studies carried out under the Gender Network under 'Additional References'.

cited above only serves to demonstrate the dire necessity of moving out of a mindset that defines human well-being in terms of simplistic instrumental indicators, like literacy. In our context, it underlines the importance of looking at some of the 'non-conventional' indicators of human well-being over and above the standard conventional ones. For both men and women, recorded levels of mental stress are very high in Kerala. High literacy levels could very well be a proximate cause of the high stress levels found in the population, but one needs to go into other environmental factors to understand the root cause of the malaise. Economic worries and job related anxieties could very well top the list among men, and gender relations could very well be one of the major defining factors for high stress levels in women.

High Female Literacy in Kerala from a Feminist Perspective

What the high literacy levels may have meant for the average woman in Kerala is explored from a feminist perspective in the paper by Devika and Mukherjee in this volume. In their assessment, historically, literacy for women in Kerala came with notions of social development that consisted of not merely the functional ability to read and write, but also how that functionality had to be used for the good of the family and society, and also the state.[20] It is not as if some women, brave and brilliant in their own right, did not question the one-sided message. Writings of women like Saraswati Amma and Antarjanam referred to in the paper, bear testimony to assertions of the self. Such assertions, though powerful and courageous in their time, had no chance of developing into an alternative paradigm. The atmosphere was inundated by ideological messages propagating 'enlightened domesticity' for women: not for the development of the self per se, but for the good of society. These messages have had such a powerful hold on the public psyche that even when the first generation of educated feminists in Kerala succeeded in negotiating some space for women in the public sphere, they could do so strictly within the bounds of the ideological framework defined for the 'good' woman.

[20]Female education, they write, meant 'not just the acquisition of literacy, but also a set of gendered attitudes and skills.' As Devika argues in another paper, the trend continued in the same vein into the post-independence years within state-sponsored programmes on family planning, supposedly designed for the benefit of the family and the state but directed exclusively to women (Devika 2003). See Devika (2007) for a fuller exposition of the theme.

This was in the role of nurturers in social sector jobs, well within the limits prescribed by the process of reforms.

Sen's 'Capability Framework'

If the line of argument advanced in these papers is valid, then perhaps one could argue that there is indeed no puzzle, no 'enigma' that marks the phenomenon of the 'woman in Kerala'. In fact, there is no reason to choose between the extremes of 'utopia' or 'dystopia' to characterize the phenomenon.[21] This disconnect arises due to the limitations of the framework that has been chosen to characterize the gender question in Kerala. Sen's capability framework, which forms the underlying basis for according a high position to literacy in human and gender development matters, is after all only a framework. Perhaps it was always meant to be one. It is indeed a very powerful framework, which may have changed the way one looks at human development, but it stops short of being a full-fledged theory. In order to make it a theory, one would need to fill in contextual specificities. As some feminist theorists have argued, one would need a theory of feminism to supplement the capability framework in order to analyse gender development issues within that framework.[22]

To recapitulate, if perception of male superiority is indeed a widely held view among Malayalee women, and if gender violence is widespread and silently borne, then there is an urgent need for careful scrutiny of the results from conventional indicator based analysis of gender development which shows the Kerala women and their position in society in an altogether different light. Conventional indicator-based analysis which depends on standard gender development indicators such as literacy and health status indicators evidently fall short, giving rise to questions about the 'enigma' of the Kerala woman.

METHODOLOGICAL ISSUES IN GENDER RESEARCH

During the course of designing this research, one has had questions that had to be probed in a multi-disciplinary setting, some that needed to be probed sequentially, and depending on the nature of the questions that needed probing, one has had to move constantly between different kinds of methodologies. This situates this body of

[21] Sharmila Sreekumar 2006.

[22] See for instance, the paper presented by Ingrid Robyens at the Conference on 'Sen's Capability Approach' at St Edmunds College, Cambridge, June 2001.

research within the arena of what has come to be known in recent times as the 'Q2 Methodology', signifying a combination of quantitative and qualitative methods.[23] From a methodological standpoint, this also opens up the possibility of linking up the analysis presented in this volume with new advances in poverty analysis through the combined use of quantitative and qualitative methods.[24] While most quantitative approaches to poverty analysis such as income-based or needs-based approaches depend heavily on objective criteria primarily derived through survey-based methods, more qualitatively oriented approaches such as participatory appraisal methods or empowerment-based approaches to poverty analysis depend primarily on qualitative information that cannot generally be aggregated like quantitative measures. It is increasingly understood that in order to make a fair assessment of the poverty situation in a particular context, one needs a mixture of both kinds of information.

These new approaches to poverty research have also paved the way for bringing in dimensions of poverty that were difficult to accommodate in purely consumption or minimum-needs based traditional approaches used earlier. Participatory methods to poverty assessment have brought in issues of social exclusion and human rights within the ambit of poverty research as important, albeit very different, dimensions of self-assessed poverty.

The notions of exclusion and human rights issues can provide a common platform for exploring an expanded notion of 'gendered poverty', which is free from the pitfalls of a generalized feminization of poverty thesis.[25]

Research in the area of women's studies under different analytical disciplines, however, has not kept pace with these developments. There is almost a clear division between quantitative and qualitative methods used in this body of research. While historians, sociologists, and social anthropologists studying gender relations primarily use qualitative methods, demographers and economists are heavily dependent on gender-disaggregated descriptive statistics. Applied statisticians and econometricians use various methods of applied statistics on such quantitative information to analyse different aspects of gender discrimination. Instances of multi-disciplinary research, especially research that combines different kinds of methodology, are not very common in gender studies. There is need for a greater

[23]For details, see http://www.q-squared.ca.

[24]Cf. Ravi Kanbur (2003.)

[25]See Chant(2006) for a critique of the 'feminization of poverty' thesis.

degree of cross-fertilization of ideas and methods between different analytical traditions in gender research. The bridging of the inter-disciplinary gaps in research methodologies has come naturally in case of the body of research presented in this volume, which evolved in the process of the evolution of the research question.

CONTENTS OF THE VOLUME

The papers, case studies and photographs included in this volume use diverse methods to find an answer to the complex question of gender relations in Kerala and to understand the enigma of the Kerala woman. This body of research questions the efficacy of conventional measures of 'gender development', when used in isolation, in capturing the essence of women's status in society.

This questioning has led to two kinds of approaches. First, an emphasis has been placed on going beyond aggregative measures to look into the available data in as disaggregated a manner as possible, the emphasis being on decompositions that would throw light on 'outliers'.[26] This was done to make it possible to identify sets of observations which may otherwise get swamped in aggregative figures and to see if there are patterns in them leading to a more focused questioning of the data.

Second, a systematic query was launched to look at gender relations in society, not simply in terms of instrumental indicators such as literacy levels, but primarily as power relations between the sexes that are upheld by societal norms. This was felt necessary in order to identify gender indicators that could go beyond contextual specificities and address the fundamental problem of the dignity of women as human beings in as context-free a manner as possible. This line of enquiry has led to a study of gender-based stress, anxiety and violence.

The first paper in Section 1 in this volume, authored by S. Irudaya Rajan and Sreerupa is an example of the first kind of query. It presents

[26]Gender disaggregated data analysis was carried out during Gender Network (I) in Bangladesh (Zohir et al. 2001), Nepal (Narula et al. 2000), India (ISST 2001), Pakistan (Siddiqui et al. 2001) and Sri Lanka (Jayaweera et al., 2000). Country-level studies on violence against women were carried out in India (Sarvanan, 2000), Sri Lanka (Wanasundara, 2000) and in South Asian countries in general (Saravanan, 2003). Edited versions of some of this material have been published in Mukhopadhyay and Sudarshan (2003). Unpublished versions of reports of Gender Network studies in the first two phases are available in nine volumes in the library of the Institute of Social Studies Trust. Also see www.isst-india.org/publications.htm. A full listing of unpublished reports in the first two phases of GN research appears as Additional References at the end of this paper.

a statistical overview of women in Kerala but goes beyond standard aggregative data to highlight areas of concern hidden behind the aggregates. This includes disturbing evidence on high infant mortality rates for female babies in recent years, sex-specific abortions, the virtual absence of social safety nets for older and widowed women, and gender-specific problems of large scale migration from Kerala in recent decades.

The second paper authored by Swapna Mukhopadhyay, Jayanti Basu, and S. Irudaya Rajan is the result of an investigation into the status of mental health of men and women in Kerala. It uses mental health indicators like the Subjective Well-Being Inventory (SUBI) and General Health Questionnaire (GHQ) widely used in applied psychological research. Based on the data generated by the Kerala Mental Health Survey (KMHS) conducted during the second phase of the Gender Network Project, it suggests the existence of a strongly negative association of orthodox/patriarchal gender ideology with the status of mental health of the population in Kerala.

The third paper by J.Devika and Avanti Mukherjee invokes the history of social reforms in the state to throw light on the process through which decades of social reforms have contributed to the shaping of the ideal Malayalee woman within the various community and caste groups in Kerala. This is a woman whose role in the family and society is cast in stone, with little room for manoeuvre, and virtually no space to break out of the mould except at her own peril. This paper stands a little apart from the other writings contained in this volume in so far as it blends the language of pure research with a flavour of feminist activism. Given the fact that a good deal of research in Women's Studies is fed on the groundswell of feminist activism, this is perhaps as it should be. The volume also includes some case studies of Kerala women conducted during the first phase of the Gender Network,[27] and several recent photographs of Kerala women taken under varied contexts.[28]

[27]The case studies included in this volume are edited versions of a subset of the case studies that appear in the Appendix to the report submitted to Gender Network by Mridul Eapen and Praveena Kodoth of the Centre for Development Studies in Trivandrum, May 2001. Dr T.K. Anandy, a sociologist based in Calicut, had taken on the responsibility of compiling the life histories of women in north and central Kerala with the help of Sandhya Chandrasekharan, Geeta and Bindu. The work in Trivandrum was carried out by Deepa Shankar of the Deprtment of Psychology, University of Kerala, with the help of N. Meera, a project assistant in the CDS project.

[28]The credit for the photographs go to Jipson Sikhera of Cochin, Kerala.

Case Studies and Photographs of Contemporary Women

Sections 2 and 3 on the case studies on women's life experiences and the photographs of contemporary Kerala women from different socio-economic backgrounds in diverse situations, supplement the analysis presented in the research papers in the first section. The case studies amply demonstrate that the average woman in Kerala is perhaps not very different from the average woman elsewhere in the country. Marriage is central to her life; her relationship with her husband defines her destiny. If the husband is not abusive, the woman considers herself fortunate. If he is alcoholic and abusive, there is little that she can do. Alcoholism among men is generally accompanied by domestic abuse of women, which is the same as elsewhere in the country.

Alcoholism in men is a phenomenon to reckon with in all states in the country, and is routinely associated with high incidence of domestic abuse of women. A decisive ranking of states in the incidence of alcoholism must wait until adequate comparative evidence is available. However, based on whatever information one has, one can say that the incidence of alcoholism in Kerala is perhaps among the highest. A complex juxtaposition of factors may have been responsible for this. High literacy levels raising career expectations, coupled with a sluggish state economy that does not generate corresponding job opportunities in the labour market, can be quite a lethal combination. Unemployment and the poverty it generates can lead to frustration that may readily feed into alcohol dependence.

Poverty can indeed exacerbate the speedy descent into alcohol addiction. But then poverty is experienced equally, if not more intensely, by the women in poor households. Why do women from these households not turn alcoholic, and abusive? Where does gender figure in this scenario? Clearly one needs deeper expert analysis of the human psyche in its various gender-differentiated manifestations in Kerala than is currently available.

Alcoholism and abusive tendencies can be further aggravated by entrenched beliefs in traditional gender norms of the male being the chief bread earner in the household, and the female, the second in the hierarchy. For men, alcohol consumption could be an instrument of proclaiming their male identity, and violence, the outward expression of cementing the male superiority. As some of the case studies indicate, the habit of alcoholism can also be imbibed from childhood experience of growing up in households with alcoholic fathers. One would need a separate study on the psyche of the alcoholic men to understand the phenomenon of alcohol addiction and the abuse of women that is almost routinely associated with it. What is apparent from the case studies however, is that, most women passively accept such abuse. They take marital violence as destiny. If it does not, then one is fortunate. If it occurs, there is not much one can do about it. This needs to be understood in the context of the perceived absence of fallback options open to the victims of marital abuse.

In this context, it is pertinent to refer to some historical factors that may have led to the increasing vulnerability of women. The steady nuclearization of households in Kerala over the last few decades, significantly propelled by state sponsored legal reforms, have concurrently altered the structure of property rights in Kerala to the distinct disadvantage of women. This, by itself, would have strengthened the gradual erosion of fallback options. In recent years, the high inflow of Gulf money into the state economy, fuelling a rise in consumerism, could also have led to this.[29]

There are reasons to believe that things have worsened over the years for the average woman in Kerala. The case studies demonstrate one thing: for the women in these interviews, the natal families did not discriminate among children on the basis of gender, at the time they were growing up. Most women report a relatively happy childhood, unless of course, there was an alcoholic father. The sex-specific restrictions on mobility and norms of behaviour came only with the onset of puberty. The situation worsened for most women only after marriage. Things have certainly changed since then. The strong evidence of sex-specific abortions in recent times, suggests that sex discrimination is widespread in the Malayalee community. Many do not want female babies to such an extent that they are willing to kill them even before they are born. The relatively poor survival rates of female babies in the under-five year age group as seen from recent SRS data from Kerala, suggests that the disaffection may have spread into the childhood of young girls as well.

A casual visitor to Kerala will notice that the average woman is distinctly 'traditional' in her behaviour. It is apparent in the manner in which she dresses, and conducts herself in public, and in the careful segregation of the sexes in the public arena. Some of the photographs

[29]Devika 2006; Palriwala 2006.

included in this volume clearly bring this out. In the Kerala Transport Corporation buses where seats are segregated for women, a woman is to be found occupying only the 'ladies' seats', and is unlikely to take a seat next to a man even if it is lying vacant and all 'ladies' seats' are already occupied. In classrooms or libraries of co-educational colleges, women students are supposed to sit together, away from their male colleagues, usually in the more crowded and ill-lit parts of the rooms. The entire community, not just the parents or husbands, joins hands in keeping a strict vigil on the young women. Authorities in educational institutions and the workplace monitor them and neighbours 'talk' (read spread rumours about the moral character of the woman) at the slightest sign of a woman straying from the straight and narrow path ordained by society. Young girls can move out alone after dark only at their own peril; the perceived risks of sexual harassment outside the carefully drawn out *'lakshman rekha'* are high. Even married couples shun going for late night movies for fear that the general public might mistake the wife for a mistress, and misbehave. From the perspective of an educated woman who can think for herself and would like to enjoy the basic freedom of making her own decisions, Kerala is far from the heaven on earth one may have been made to believe.

CONCLUDING OBSERVATIONS

It is a pity that the feminist movement in Kerala, until perhaps very recently, failed to connect with working class women within the Left movement. As Devika and Mukherjee point out, women's constituency had been conspicuously absent not merely within the mainstream Congress-dominated political movements in the pre-independence years but equally so from the agenda of the Left. While the first generation educated feminists were by and large distant from the travails of working class women, the perception of the leadership in the Left movement in the state was dominated by undifferentiated class concerns. Gender was not even considered to be a problem of any importance. The ambiguities created by this blinkered view of social reality was devastating, especially for the women who may have been exposed to the empowering potentials of Left-leaning ideas, as the life story of one of the women included in the case study section succinctly reveals. The Left movement in the state could have been a natural ally of feminism, since both ideologies are built on the premise of unequal power relations in society. Historically, by turning a blind eye to gender-based inequities, all political parties in the state have not merely denied women a legitimate foothold in the political arena, but have lost a potential for their own growth and regeneration as well.

Benevolent patriarchy has had a long history in Kerala, and social reformers have been especially active. The strength and resilience that this ideology has enjoyed over the years is apparent from the essential similarities in outlook shared by pairs of Kerala women from two generations separated by decades, as shown in a recent publication (Devika 2006). As has been pointed out earlier in this chapter, instead of signs of abatement, some of the mutations of the ideology that are being manifested in recent years are gaining strength at an alarming rate. Apart from domestic violence, there is clear evidence of rampant sex-selective abortions of the unborn female foetus all across Kerala. Evidence suggests that it is more widespread especially among the more affluent and educated households in the southern parts of the state. Clearly, it can happen only with the connivance of the woman. One needs to understand why women, even or especially the educated ones are willing partners in this act. Why does Kerala—that is supposed to be the haven of gender development in India, and has had a long record of high sex ratios in accordance with the normal biological outcomes prevalent in gender sensitive societies—display such an upsurge in the preference for a male child? The example of Kerala shows that neither high female literacy nor higher economic affluence of the household can guarantee gender equality. High levels of gender development in terms of conventional instrumental indicators can co-exist with significant gender-based violence.

In exploring the gender question in Kerala, the Gender Network has sought to find an explanation for this seeming paradox, and backed by multi-disciplinary research, has provided some plausible answers. In a way, understanding the 'enigma' of the Kerala woman has been central to our research since it has involved the contentious issue of defining 'women's status'. The Kerala case clearly demonstrates that if one has to choose one indicator for this elusive factor, it has to be in terms of the human dignity accorded to women by the society she lives in, and not in terms of some instrumental indicator like literacy which may, for a variety of reasons, fail to perform its transformative task of empowering the individual.

The research reflected in this volume suggests that, contrary to received wisdom, the woman of Kerala is yet to earn her 'freedom'.

Prometheus-like, she needs to break free from her shackles before she can realize the full potential of her capabilities.

REFERENCES

Arendt, Hannah, 1970, *On Violence*, New York: Harvest Books.

Centre for Women Development Studies, 2002, *Crimes against Women: Bondage and Beyond*, New Delhi: CWDS.

Chant, Sylvia, 2006, 'Rethinking the "Feminizaton of Poverty" in Relation to Aggregate Gender Indices', *Journal of Human Development*, Vol. 7, No. 2, July.

Devika, J., 2007, *'En-Gendering Individuals: The Language of Re-forming in Early Twentieth Century Keralam'*, New Delhi: Orient Longman.

_____, (ed. and trans.), 2005, *Her Self: Early Writings on Gender by Malayalee Women 1898–1938*, Kolkata: Stree.

_____, 2002, 'Family Planning as "Liberation": The Ambiguities of Emancipation from Biology', *Keralam*, July; working paper 335, Thiruvananthapuram: Centre for Development Studies.

_____, 2002, 'Domesticating Malayalees: Family Planning, the Nation and Home-Centred Anxieties in Mid-20th Century Keralam,' October; working paper 340, Thiruvananthapuram: Centre for Development Studies.

Doniger, Wendy, 1992, *The Laws of Manu* (Translation of 'Manu Smriti' from Sanskrit), London: Penguin Books.

Dreze, Jean and Sen, A.K., 1995, *India: Economic Development and Social Opportunity*, Delhi: Oxford University Press.

Eapen, Mridul and Kodoth, Praveena, 2001, 'Demystifying the High Status of Women in Kerala: An Attempt to Understand the Contradiction in Social Development', report submitted to New Delhi: Institute of Social Studies Trust under MIMAP-Gender Network Project (Phase I).

Economic and Political Weekly, 1996, Special Issue on Gender and Development Indices, Vol. 31, No. 43, 26 October.

International Centre for Research on Women (ICRW), 2000, 'Domestic Violence in India: A Summary Report of a Multi-Site Household Survey', report submitted to the International Centre for Research on Women, Washington D.C.

Kanbur, Ravi, (ed.) 2003, *Q-Squared: Qualitative and Quantitative Methods of Poverty Appraisal*, New Delhi: Permanent Black.

Mohamed, E., Rajan, S.I., Kumar, K. Anil and Mohammed, P.M. Saidu, 2002, 'Gender and Mental Health in Kerala', (Kerala Mental Health Survey), report submitted to the Institute of Social Studies Trust under MIMAP-Gender Network Project (Phase II).

Mukherjee, Chandan, Rustogi, Preet and Krishnaji, N., 2001, 'Crimes against Women in India: Analysis of Official Statistics', *Economic and Political Weekly*, Vol. 36, No. 43.

Mukhopadhyay, Swapna, 1998, 'The Proposed Gender Planning Network for South and South East Asia: An Expository Note', in The Genesis and Design of the MIMAP-Gender Network. Vol. I. of Gender Network Reports.

——, 2003, 'What is New about Gender Bias?' in Swapna Mukhopadhyay and Ratna Sudarshan (eds.), *Tracking Gender Equity under Economic Reforms: Continuity and Change in South Asia*, New Delhi: Kali for Women & IDRC.

—— and Nandi, Rajib, 2006, 'Unpacking the Assumption of Gender Neutrality: Akshaya Project of the Kerala IT Mission in India', *Gender, Technology and Development (forthcoming)*.

—— and Savithri, R., 1998, *Poverty, Gender and Reproductive Choice: An Analysis of Linkages*, New Delhi: Manohar Publications.

—— and Sudarshan, Ratna, (eds.), 2003, *Tracking Gender Equity under Economic Reforms: Continuity and Change in South Asia*, New Delhi: Kali for Women & International Development Research Centre (IDRC), Canada.

Palriwala, Rajni, 2006, (2006) 'Reaffirming the Anti-dowry Struggle' in Srimati Basu (ed.), *Dowry and Inheritence: Issues in Contemporary Feminism*, London: Zed Books.

Pandey, Gyanendra, 2005, *Routine Violence: Nations, Fragments and Histories*, California: Stanford University Press.

Robyens, Ingrid, 2004, 'Sen's Capability Approach and Feminist Concerns', Paper presented at the conference on 'Sen's Capability Approach', Cambridge, 2001, Revised version, April.

Saravanan, Sheela, 2003, 'Manifestation of Gender Bias in South Asia: An Overview', Report prepared at the Institute of Social Studies Trust, New Delhi under MIMAP-Gender Network Project (Phase I).

Sen, Amartya, 2000, *Development as Freedom*, New Delhi: Oxford University Press.

Sonpar, Shobna and Kapur, Ravi, 2003, 'Non-conventional Indicators of Gender Disparities under Structural Reforms', in Swapna Mukhopadhyay and Ratna Sudarshan (eds.), *Tracking Gender Equity under Economic Reforms: Continuity and Change in South Asia*, New Delhi: Kali for Women & IDRC.

Sreekumar, Sharmila, 2006, 'The Land of Gender Paradox ? Getting Past the Commonsense of Contemporary Kerala' Paper presented in the Gender Network Conference in Jaipur, India, 1–4 February.

UNIFEM, 2000, *Progress of the World's Women 2000*, UNIFEM, New York.

ADDITIONAL REFERENCES

This section provides a full listing of unpublished reports of studies carried out under the Gender Network Project in Phase I (1998–2001) and Phase II (2001–03). These have been put together in nine volumes and are available in the ISST library.

The Genesis and Design of the Mimap-Gender Network, Vol. I

ISST, 2000, 'Research Agenda of the MIMAP Gender Network: A Bird's Eye View', ISST, chapter 5.

Mukhopadhyay, Swapna, 1998, 'What is New about Gender Bias?', ISST, chapter 1.

____, 1998, 'The Proposed Gender Planning Network for South and South East Asia: An Expository Note', ISST, chapter 2.

____ and Ratna Sudarshan, 1998, 'Gender Discrimination and its Indicators: A Research Agenda', ISST, chapter 3.

____, 2000, 'MIMAP Gender Network: Background and an Account of Work in Progress', ISST, chapter 4.

Major Conventional Gender Indicators in South Asia, Vol. II

Chaudhuri, Salma Zohir, Sharifa Begum and Basher Abul, (BIDS), Bangladesh, 2001, 'Changes in the Conventional Indicators During Adjustment in Bangladesh', ISST, chapter 3.

ISST, 2000, 'Major Conventional Indicators in India: India Country Report, Vol. I', ISST, chapter 1.

Jayaweera, Swarna, (CENWOR), Sri Lanka, 2000, 'Major Conventional Indicators in Sri Lanka', ISST, chapter 4.

Niraula, Bhanu, and Luitel Samira, (ARROSC), Nepal, 2000, 'Major Conventional Indicators in Nepal', ISST, chapter 2.

Saravanan, Sheela, 2003, 'Manifestation of Gender Bias in South Asia: An Overview', ISST, chapter 5.

Violence against Women, Vol. III

CENWOR Sri Lanka, 2001, 'Gender Dimensions of Macro-Economic Reforms: Gender Roles and Relations in Sri Lanka', ISST, chapter 4.

Kapur, R.L., and Sonpar, Shobna, 1999, 'Non-Conventional Indicators: Gender Disparities under Structural Reforms', ISST, chapter 1.

Saravanan, Sheela, 2000, 'Violence Against Women in India', ISST, chapter 2.

Wanasundera, Leelangi, (CENWOR), Sri Lanka, 2000, 'Country Report on Violence Against Women in Sri Lanka', ISST, chapter 3.

Gender Dimension of Macroeconomic Reforms: Reports on Household Surveys of Workers in Export Processing Zones, Vol. IV

CENWOR, Sri Lanka, 2000, 'Gender Dimensions of Macro-Economic Reforms: Employment, Underemployment, and Unemployment in Sri Lanka', ISST, chapter 4.

ISST, 2001, 'A Report on the Household Survey of Workers from EPZs and EOUs in India, India Country Report Vol. II', ISST, chapter 1.

Siddiqui, Rehana, Hamid, Shahnaz, Soomro, G. Yasin, Siddiqui, Rizwana, and Akhtar, Naeem, Pakistan Institute of Development Economics (PIDE), Pakistan, 2001, 'Gender Dimension on the Impact of Macroeconomic Policies (A Case Study of Pakistan)', ISST, chapter 2.

Zohir, Salma Chaudhuri, Bangladesh Institute of Development Studies (BIDS), Bangladesh, 2001, 'Gender Balance in the EPZ: A Socio-Economic Study of Dhaka Export Processing Zone in Bangladesh', ISST, chapter 3.

——, and Yunus, Mohammad, Bangladesh Institute of Development Studies (BIDS), Bangladesh, 2001, 'Household Response: A Study on Households of Female EPZ Workers in Bangladesh', ISST, chapter 5.

Modelling Gender: Review of Evidence and Theories, Vol. V

Dauphin, Anyck, (CECI), Canada, 2001, 'Gender and Intra-Household Decision Making: A Review of Theories and their Relevance for Micro-Modeling', ISST, chapter 1.

Fontana, Marzia, International Food Policy Research Institute, Washington D.C., 2003, 'Modeling the Effects of Trade on Women at Work and at Home: A Comparative Perspective', ISST, chapter 3.

Sinha, Anushree, and N., Sangeeta, National Council of Applied Economic Research (NCAER), India, 2001, 'Gender in a Macro-Economic Framework: A CGE Model Analysis', ISST, chapter 2.

——, Siddiqui, K.A., Munjal, Poonam, and Subudhi, Sonali, National Council of Applied Economic Research (NCAER) India, 2003, 'Impact of Globalization on Indian Women Workers: A Study with CGE Analysis', ISST, chapter 4.

Status of Women in Kerala, Vol. VI

Eapen, Mridul, and Kodoth, Praveena, Centre for Development Studies (CDS) India, 2001, 'Demystifying the High Status of Women in Kerala: An Attempt to Understand the Contradiction in Social Development', ISST, chapter 1.

Mohamed, E., Rajan, S.I., Anil Kumar, K., and Mohammed, P.M. Saidu, Ansar Hospital, Trissur, India, 2003, 'Gender and Mental Health in Kerala', ISST, chapter 2.

Gender and Poverty, Vol. VII

Jayaweera, Swarna, Sanmugum, Thana, and Amarasuriya, Harini, Centre for Women's Research (CENWOR), Sri Lanka, 2003, 'Gender and Poverty in Selected Locations in Sri Lanka', ISST, chapter 5.

Mukhopadhyay, Swapna, and Ghatak, Shambhu, 2003, 'Analysing Linkages between Gender and Poverty: A Methodological Note', ISST, chapter 1.

Mustafa Mujeri, Bangladesh Institute of Development Studies (BIDS), Bangladesh, 2003, 'Gender Issues at the Local Level: Summary Results of a Pilot Survey in Bangladesh', ISST, chapter 2.

Reyes, Celia M., P. Asirot, Jasminda, C. Ilarde Kenneth, et al., DLSU, Philippines, 2003, 'Gender and Poverty: The Case of Philippines. Vol. I & II', ISST, chapter 4.

Sharma, Ram K., and Manasa Thakurathi, National Labour Academy (NLA), Nepal, 2003, 'Including Non-Conventional Gender Indicators in Local Planning in Nepal', ISST, chapter 6.

Siddiqui, Rehana, and Hamid, Shahnaz, Pakistan Institute of Development Studies (PIDE), Pakistan, 2003, 'Correlates of Poverty: Gender Dimensions',ISST, chapter 3.

Gender Differences in the Impact of Economic Reforms: The Case of Retrenched Worker Households, Vol. VIII

Jayaweera, Swarna, Sanmugam, Thana, and Amarasuriya Harini, (CENWOR), Sri Lanka, 2003, ISST, chapter 2.

Mukhopadhyay, Swapna, Bhattacharya, Rina, Nandi, Rajib, and Swarankar, Ranjan, ISST, 2003, 'Gender Differences in the Impact of Retrenchment: A Comparative Study of Delhi and West Bengal in India', ISST, chapter 1.

Gender, Employment and Technology, Vol. IX

Mitter, Swasti, U.K., 2003, 'Exploring Employment and Livelihood Opportunities for Women in the ICT Sector in South and Southeast Asian Countries', ISST, chapter 2.

Senapaty, Manju, Ministry of Commerce, Government of India, 2001, 'Trade, Gender and Employment Issues', ISST, chapter 1.

chapter two

Gender Disparity in Kerala
A Critical Reinterpretation

S. Irudaya Rajan and Sreerupa

INTRODUCTION

Kerala's performances in terms of demographic transition, social and health-related indicators are well documented. A matrilineal system, social reforms, high literacy and educational levels have played a significant role in raising the position of women in Kerala society, enabling them to make outstanding gains and match the performance of men. As a result the state has always had good ranking in the Human Development and Gender Empowerment Indices compared to the rest of the states in India. Beyond what these indicators reveal, however, there are certain areas where gender disparity still persists. This paper assesses the various facets and extent of disparities between females and males in migration, ageing, literacy, education and employment. It also discusses certain emerging challenges facing women in contemporary Kerala society.

Historically, women in the northern states of India have experienced extreme gender discrimination whereas women in the southern states have displayed more egalitarian gender development indicators (Dyson and Moore 1983; Miller 1981). In this context, the 'Kerala Model of Development'[1] is upheld as an example for other states to emulate. It is heralded not only for the state's achievements with

[1]Kerala's accomplishments show that the well-being of the people in terms of demographic, education, health and other social indicators can be achieved at a low cost and with a low per capita income.

respect to certain socio-demographic and health indicators but also because these gains did not appear to come at gender unequal terms. The Kerala woman made outstanding gains in the spheres of health and education, matching the performance of men in the state in terms of these conventional development indicators. Kerala's gender equal social development outcomes seemed to follow from the 'high status' enjoyed by women in the state and their central role, historically, in social development (Jeffery 1992). It is often claimed that gender discrimination is low in Kerala. Indeed it is, if one goes by the conventional indicators and measures, and adopts a comparative perspective vis-à-vis other Indian states. A good example of such a measure is the Gender Development Index (GDI) developed by UNDP in 1995 to assess the inequality in attainments between males and females, as shown by human development indicators. Among the Indian states, Kerala topped the Gender Development Index indicating a gender equal society.[2] Its long tradition of a matrilineal system, social reforms, high literacy and educational levels has played a significant role in improving the condition of women. However, a closer look at some of these conventional indicators reveals disquieting evidence that although gender parity has been achieved in select indicators there is much to be desired in terms of equity in gender relations. It appears, therefore, that only the practical needs of the female population have been taken care of without a full-bodied attempt at gender transformation or questioning of conventional gender roles. This becomes clear from the results of studies focusing on gender empowerment indicators that signify power and autonomy in terms of household decision making, mobility and so on. The study revealed that Kerala trailed a number of states like Gujarat, Tamil Nadu, Punjab and Goa with much lower levels of female literacy (IIPS 2000).

In this context, there is further evidence available with regard to certain non-conventional indicators[3] which show growing gender disparity, like the rising visibility of gender based violence, mental illness among women, and the rapid growth and spread of dowry and dowry-related crimes (Kodoth and Eapen 2005). Many scholars

[2]Available Gender Disparity Index shows that Kerala stood first in 1981 (0.872 points) and reached second position in 1991 (0.825 points).

[3]See paper titled 'Non-conventional indicators of gender disparities under the structural reforms' by Shobna Sonpar and Ravi Kapur. http://www.isst-india.org/PDF/Kapoor%20and%20Sonpar.pdf

have drawn attention to the ways in which women's status in Kerala has declined since the middle of the twentieth century (see for example Gulati and Rajan 1997; Saradamoni 1994, 1999). In the light of such events, this paper assesses the extent of disparities between females and males in terms of certain demographic and socio-economic indicators. Further, it discusses certain emerging challenges facing women in contemporary Kerala society with the understanding that neither the relative high status of women nor the developmental achievements made by women are a static cultural feature to remain unaffected by socio-economic changes.

The study is explorative in nature and uses secondary data from various published sources. This paper has two main sections followed by concluding observations from the study. The first section provides a critical discussion of some aspects of gender disparity in the social development in Kerala. This section assesses gender differentials in the sex ratio, age at marriage, trends in fertility and contraception, life expectancy, education, work participation and unemployment. The second section explores the future crises in gender parity with respect to certain emergent issues in Kerala society such as ageing, migration, changing juvenile sex ratio and rising crime rates. The concluding observations of the study are presented in the final section.

SOME ASPECTS OF GENDER DISPARITY IN SOCIAL DEVELOPMENT IN KERALA

Kerala's social development trajectory has been hailed for its gender equitable outcomes and its social development indicators stand out from that of the rest of the country due to their apparent gender parity, in favourable sex ratio, high age at marriage among women, better female life expectancy, control over fertility, mass female literacy and educational attainments. In this section of the paper we will engage in a critical examination of each of these social development outcomes in an attempt to demystify the gender disparities associated with them.

It appears that male dominated migration from Kerala may explain, at least, in part, the favourable sex ratio in the state; adjusting for the same reduces the female advantage substantially. At the same time there is little evidence that the high age at marriage among women in Kerala has resulted in better terms of marriage for them or increased participation in the workforce. It may be associated with improvements in the level of female education, but the pursuit of higher education among women seems to be highly gendered with very diverse social expectations from female and male education. This is also manifested in skewed workforce participation rates. Further, female literacy and higher education seems to have failed to unsettle the dominant gender norms in matters relating to fertility control and the use of contraception.

Sex Ratio

> 'A key indicator—and perhaps the most illustrative summary measure—of the historical status of women in Kerala ... is the sex ratio'
>
> (Ramachandran 1996)

Kerala's sex ratio is unique among the Indian states as it is the only one with an excess of females and the only one where this excess has grown consistently during the past century (Rajan and Aliyar 2005: 171). Kerala has a female-male ratio of 1058 as compared to 933 for the rest of India as per the 2001 census (Figure 2.1). The low female-male ratio in other parts of India has been seen as an evidence of female foeticide, relative neglect and a survival disadvantage among females resulting from highly unequal gender relations (Dreze and Sen 1995: 142). On the other hand the survival advantage of women in Kerala is linked to the 'distinguished history of a more liberated position of women' (Dreze and Sen 1995: 142).

Figure 2.1: Sex Ratio in Kerala and India, 1911–2001

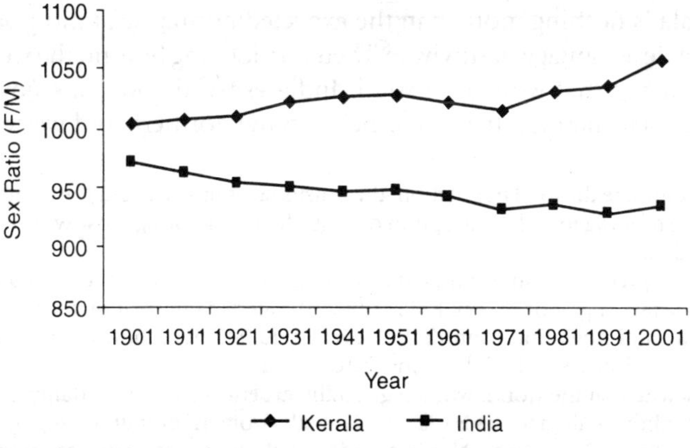

Source: Compiled by the authors from various Census reports
Note: Sex ratio is expressed as number of females per 1000 males

The sex ratio in a country is determined by the interplay of various factors such as sex differentials in mortality, sex selective migration, sex ratio at birth and sex differentials in enumeration at the time of the Census. There are certain methodological problems with the calculation of the sex ratio, as the census does not adjust for male dominated migration in Kerala.[4] A recent survey has estimated that there are 1.8 million emigrants from Kerala of whom a majority of 84 percent are male (Zachariah and Rajan 2004). Hence Kerala's high female-male ratio may be partly explained by the high levels of male out migration.

Kerala Migration Survey[5] (KMS) estimates show that there are 953 males per 1000 females in Kerala. Thus according to KMS, there is a deficit of 47 males per 1000 population in the state. However, after including the emigrants and out migrants from the state there are 1043 males per 1000 females. Thus, the deficit of 47 males turns into an excess of 43 males. Had there been no migration from Kerala, the number of males would have been greater than the number of females—similar to the pattern in other states in India. If this conclusion is valid, the major factor behind the favourable sex ratio in Kerala is not lower mortality rates but lower female migration rates (Zachariah et al. 2003:172). Moreover, this argument is further substantiated by the very large deficit of males in the working age groups. For example, the sex ratio in the age group 30–34 years in Malappuram district was only 597; and that in the age group 35–39 years was even lower at 560. In both these age groups the deficit of men was more than 400 per 1000 population in Malappuram.

Meanwhile it is important to note that even a favourable sex ratio in Kerala is nothing more than the expected normal sex ratio given the female advantage in survival.[6] Therefore looking beyond the well-accepted fact that women in south India especially Kerala enjoy a better social standing than their peers in the northern and western

[4]To estimate the total population, the census takes into account the number of people residing in a place at a point of time, thereby ignoring those who have migrated out.

[5]A comprehensive survey undertaken by Centre for Development Studies, entitled Kerala Migration Survey, KMS (1998–9) collected information on various dimensions of migration from Kerala covering 10,000 households at random from all the districts and taluks in the state.

[6]Elsewhere in the world, women generally experience lower mortality than men at almost all ages (Visaria 2002) with women outnumbering men substantially in Europe and North America, with an average ratio of around 1.05 (Dreze and Sen 1995).

states, we need to question the wisdom of accepting a favourable sex ratio as an evidence of gender equality in Kerala society.

Age at Marriage

The state has always enjoyed a relatively high age at marriage and in 1947, although the mean age at marriage of girls in Kerala was about 15–16 years, it was higher than any other state in India (Zachariah 1998). Significant differences have existed in the age at marriage of females in Kerala and India. The mean age at marriage of Kerala women was 22.2 years in 2001 with insignificant rural-urban difference. On the other hand, the age at marriage of females in India was only 19.8 years with a considerable rural urban difference (Table 2.1).

In other words, only one fourth of all women ages 20–49 years

Table 2.1 Mean Age at Marriage among Females, 1991–2000

Year	*Kerala*			*India*		
	Total	*Rural*	*Urban*	*Total*	*Rural*	*Urban*
1991	22.0	22.0	22.2	19.5	19.2	20.6
1995	21.7	21.8	21.7	19.4	19.0	20.3
2000	22.2	22.1	22.7	19.8	19.4	21.1

Source: Office of the Registrar General (SRS division), New Delhi

(14% in urban areas and 29% in rural areas) were married below the age of 18 years in Kerala, whereas, in the rest of India, 61% of the women in ages 20–49 (69% rural and 41% urban) had married before turning 18 (IIPS 2000). The proportion of Kerala girls marrying after 21 years is 63% while this is only 25.9% at the national level (Government of Kerala 2004).

Though the age at marriage among Kerala females is high compared to India, there are considerable differentials among caste and religious groups and women of diverse educational attainments. For example, the difference between the ages at marriage of illiterate women and those who complete high school is about five years (Rajan and Aliyar 2005: 174). Generally rise in the age of marriage is attributed to improvements in the levels of female education especially in Kerala's context. Meanwhile, concerns have been raised about whether the rising age at marriage among females can be attributed entirely to the improvement in the levels of female education. Alternative hypotheses have also been suggested, such as increase in the average age at marriage of males triggering a rise in the average age at marriage of females (Krishnan 1976). Further investigation is, therefore, needed to ascertain whether the increase in the age at marriage has been on account of women's empowerment achieved through better education, or is simply the outcome of conforming to the marital norm of women not marrying older men. Moreover, the belief that high age at marriage is usually associated with better terms of marriage for women and diversified livelihood options, needs to be further investigated in Kerala's context.

Fertility and Contraception

Even during the early 1950s Kerala had a lower fertility level than the all India average. The initial difference in fertility levels was almost entirely due to the higher age at marriage among Kerala women. However, the large difference in fertility levels that we see now arises mainly from a greater use of contraception (Zachariah 1998). Kerala's birth rate had started declining by the middle of the 1950s and gained momentum in the late 1960s. The Crude Birth Rate (CBR) in 1951–61 was 43.9, declining steadily in 1971–81 to 28.1, and falling further in 2001 to 16.9 per 1000 population.

Fertility transition in Kerala is a unique event in the demographic history of the sub-continent as it took just about a generation to reach a level significantly lower than that of the replacement (Zachariah 1998). From about six children per woman in the early 1950s, the number of children per woman had declined to 1.7 by 1993 and to 1.6 in 2001 (Guilmoto and Rajan 2002). Kerala's advantage in fertility decline has many reasons. It is most likely that the state attained low fertility through many conventional social and health correlates which include high overall and female literacy, increased mean age at marriage, successful implementation of maternal and child health care programmes that include universal immunization for better child survival, effective administration and reach of official family planning programmes (Krishnan 1976; Ratcliffe 1978; Bhat and Rajan 1990; Zachariah et al. 1994; Zachariah and Rajan 1997; Zachariah 1998).

Fertility decline has certain inherent health advantages for women, since they are relieved from the drudgery of continuous child bearing and rearing, not to mention the dangers of repeated pregnancy and high maternal mortality (Dreze and Sen 1995: 167). Also compressing the reproductive phase to a smaller span during the initial years of marriage provides an opportunity for them to get involved in economically productive activities. Therefore it is often associated with enhancement of women's status and voice (ibid.). To attribute any more gender benefits to the phenomenon might be dangerous as evident from Kerala society where the decline in fertility hasn't resulted in a concomitant improvement in the female work participation rate as discussed later in this chapter.

In Kerala as elsewhere, family planning programmes were instrumental in bringing down fertility rates. The Second National Family Health Survey (1998–9) shows that all currently married women in Kerala know at least one method of family planning and 77% have used a family planning method. Among currently married women in the age group 15–49 years, the current contraceptive prevalence is 64% in Kerala, compared to 48% at the national level (IIPS 2000). However what goes unsaid is that the whole burden of contraception has fallen unilaterally on the women. For instance, 48.5% of the women were sterilized as against only 2.5% of the men in Kerala. At the national level, this proportion is 34.2% and 1.9% respectively. What these statistics reveal is that the gender imbalance in the adoption of the family planning programmes in Kerala is as high as elsewhere in the country. There is no evidence of a shared responsibility between men and women in the success of demographic transition even in Kerala. Significantly the greater utilization of contraceptives among women does not necessarily reflect a greater control over fertility decisions. In short, the dominant gender norms in matters relating to fertility control and use of contraception have not been challenged in a society believed to be gender equal, with a large educated female population.[7]

Education

Scholarly works on literacy in Kerala have shown that, historically, a favourable cultural condition[8] for female literacy has prevailed in the state.[9] Even in the mid-nineteenth century, girls in Kerala enjoyed

[7]See also Devika (2002), 'Domesticating Malayalees: Family Planning, the Nation and Home-centred Anxieties in mid-20th century Keralam', October, working Paper 340, Thiruvananthapuram: Centre for Development Studies.

[8]In a traditionally matrilineal society, women in Kerala did not face the social barriers typical of many other Indian states.

[9]For a more detailed discussion on matriliny and its positive fallout on female literacy, see Gough (1961) and Jeffery (1992).

a level of education not available in any other part of the country. However the major impetus to literacy among women in Kerala is a recent phenomenon. It was not until the 1960s that the majority of females became literate (Ramachandran 1996). Today, Kerala is a leading state in male as well as female literacy.

Kerala's overall literacy rate (among population aged seven years and above) was 90.92% compared to the national average of 64.84% in 2001 (Table 2.2). The male and female literacy rates in Kerala were 94.2% and 87.86% respectively in 2001, which is a marked improvement from the level of 58.35% and 36.43% around the time of independence. In Kerala, the female literacy rate has increased by two and a half times whereas the male-female gap in literacy rate (difference between male and female literacy rate) has declined from 22% to 6.3% during last fifty years.[10] Conversely this gap has widened in India from 18.3% to 21.6% indicating a widening gender gap in terms of literacy rates. Literacy is regarded as one of the important indicators of women's 'status', affecting fertility and mortality outcomes

Table 2.2 Sex Differentials in Literacy Rates in India and Kerala 1901–2001 (percentages)

Year	*Kerala*				*India*			
	Persons	*Males*	*Females*	*Male–female gap*	*Persons*	*Males*	*Females*	*Male-female gap*
1901	11.14	19.15	3.15	16.00	5.39	9.83	0.60	9.23
1911	13.31	22.25	4.43	17.82	5.92	10.56	1.05	9.51
1921	19.20	27.88	10.26	17.62	7.16	12.21	1.81	10.40
1931	21.34	30.89	11.00	19.89	9.50	15.59	2.93	12.66
1941	NA	NA	NA	NA	16.1	24.90	7.30	17.60
1951	47.18	58.35	36.43	21.92	18.30	27.16	8.86	18.30
1961	55.08	64.89	45.56	19.33	28.30	40.39	15.33	25.06
1971	69.75	77.13	62.53	14.60	34.45	45.95	21.97	23.98
1981	78.85	84.56	73.36	11.20	43.67	56.50	29.85	26.65
1991	89.81	93.62	86.17	7.45	52.21	64.13	39.29	24.84
2001	90.92	94.20	87.86	6.34	64.84	75.26	53.67	21.59

Source: Compiled by the authors from various Census reports

[10]The decline in the gender disparity in literacy was not consistent over the last hundred years. Under the British rule the gap seemed to widen but showed a sharp decline in the post-independence period.

(Mason 1985). Hence Kerala's remarkable achievements in social indicators like fertility decline and improvement in health outcomes were also seen to be rooted in the achievement of mass female literacy.

Apart from literacy, Kerala also occupies a prime position among the rest of the states in educational expansion with a wide spatial coverage.[11] Studies on gender differentials in educational attainment across Indian states have found that females have lower educational attainment compared to males (Raza and Agarwal 1984; Tilak and Bhatt 1989; Unni 1996). However Kerala has the enviable achievement of near universalization of primary education for both girls and boys (Nair 1989; Ambili 1999) and extremely low levels of school drop-out rates, bridging the gender gap in school education almost entirely (Nair 1999: 1). Interestingly the gender pattern of the school drop-out rate is adverse to boys with 18.93% of them dropping out as compared to 9.82% of girls before reaching the tenth standard in 2002-3 (Achin 2005:545).

In 1991, the enrolment rate of children between the ages of 6 and 11 years is 91.2% (91.3 for males and 91.1 for females) whereas at the national level this proportion is 51.2% (56.6 for males and 45.4 for females; Government of India 2002a). It clearly points towards greater gender equality in Kerala in terms of school access as well as enrolment in the younger ages. Kerala had the highest proportion of enrolment of girl students in school education in India in 2003–4 (Government of Kerala 2004: 408). Table 2.3 reveals that, in 2003–4, out of the 48.94 lakh students enrolled in schools, 24.01 lakh (49.1%) are girls.

Table 2.3 Sex-wise Distribution of Enrolment in Different Layers of Schools 1971–72 to 2003–2004

Year	*Lower Primary*		*Upper Primary*		*High School*		*Total*	
	Boys	*Girls*	*Boys*	*Girls*	*Boys*	*Girls*	*Boys*	*Girls*
1971–72	52.3	47.7	53.6	46.4	52.1	47.9	52.6	47.4
1981–82	51.6	48.4	52.4	47.6	51.3	48.7	51.8	48.2
1991–92	51.3	48.7	51.4	48.6	50.0	50.0	51.0	49.0
2001–02	50.7	49.3	51.8	48.2	50.4	49.6	51.0	49.0
2003–04	50.4	49.6	51.7	48.3	50.7	49.3	50.9	49.1

Source: Directorate of Public Instruction, Trivandrum

[11]The state has one lower primary school for every square km of area and one high school for every four square km and the facilities are more or less evenly distributed between rural and urban areas (NCERT 1998).

A look at the male-female enrolment rates over the years indicates that the gender gap in school education has almost been wiped out in Kerala. The picture at the all India level is a stark contrast with much lower levels of enrolment and higher drop-out rates among girls as compared to boys (Ambili 1999) (see table A2.1 in the appendix).

The enrolment rate of girls in both higher secondary and vocational higher secondary education is a healthy figure greater than 50% in 2002–3. However, the proportion of enrolment of girls in Navodaya and ICSE schools is on the lower side at 41.6% each (see table A2.2 in the appendix). A quick look at the graduate and post graduate level courses reveals a predominance of girl students with about two-thirds of the students enrolled in graduate courses and almost three-fourths in post graduate courses being girls (see table A2.3 in the appendix).

A snapshot of the educational attainments of the state reveals a very rosy picture with high levels of male and female literacy, near universalization of primary education among both boys and girls with a very low school drop-out rate among girls and a female advantage in sections of higher education. However a critical look at the pattern of education pursued after schooling, through a gender lens, reveals that the courses that have a larger intake of girls are those that lead to 'suitable' professions for women, from the point of view of their familial responsibilities (Eapen and Kodoth 2004).

What is interesting in the field of higher education is the overwhelming number of females at graduate and postgraduate levels in general arts and science courses, which are not necessarily aimed at equipping an individual with skills to become economically productive. The preponderance of women in such courses gives strength to the argument that higher education could be seen as a means to further 'marriageability' of girls, by enabling them to make better wives and mothers and a potential contributors to the economic well-being of the family (Eapen and Kodoth 2004). Some data on the sex-wise break up of enrolment in higher education shows a preponderance of women in post-graduate courses in Social Work and Education (MSW: 78.6% and M.Ed: 61.8%) which have traditionally been seen as feminine fields of work. At the same time, areas like research, management and new age professional courses like computer application see a predominance of male students (Table 2.4).

In the case of professional courses like medicine and engineering, a noteworthy feature is that though there is no significant variation

Table 2.4 Sex-wise Enrolments at Higher Education in Kerala, 2003

Courses	*Total*	*Boys*	*Girls*	*Percentage of females*
M.Phil	276	153	123	44.60
MSW	210	45	165	78.60
MBA	203	116	87	42.80
MCA	169	85	84	49.70
M. Ed	34	13	21	61.80

Source: Government of Kerala (2004a)
Note: Estimates are as on 30 September 2003

between the sexes in terms of the rate at which students qualify for the entrance examinations, glaring gender differences emerge at application stage with a marked preference among female students for the medical entrance examination as compared to engineering. Data shows that 61% of the students appearing for the medical entrance exams are females as compared to only 44% for engineering. The gender difference widens at the stage of enrolment, for example, in the case of engineering, the percentage of females enrolled is only slightly more than one third. A closer look reveals a further gender segregation in specializations taken up. The enrolment of girls is abysmally low in certain specializations like mechanical (1%), mechanical-production (5%), applied electronics and instrumentation (10%), instrumentation and control (18.75%), production cum plant (20%) and industrial engineering (25%). Bio-medical (58.7%) and electronics and instrumentation (57.1%) engineering are the two branches of engineering with more than 50% female enrolment. This evidence throws light on the persistent gender disparities and invisible entry barriers for females in certain professional courses and specializations, particularly in the field of engineering.

Similarly in the field of technical education, which is supposed to equip a student with skills to improve his/her earning capacity, there seems to be clear gender disparity (Table 2.5). The total number of students enrolled in polytechnics in 2002–3, for various diploma courses was 28,140 of which 20,315 were boys (72.2%) and 7825, girls (27.8%). Similarly in technical high schools, in 2001–2, the enrolment of boys was 78.1% as compared to only 21.9% for girls (Government of Kerala 2004a). In the low-end job oriented technical educational institutions during the 1990s, the intake of girls was below 10% in technical schools, 13% and 23% in Industrial Training Institutes (ITIs) and Industrial Training Centres (ITCs). Data on trade-

Table 2.5 Course-wise Enrolment of Students in Engineering Courses, 2002–03

Courses	*Total*	*Boys*	*Girls*	*Percentage of girls*
Civil Engineering	2408	1250	1158	48.10
Chemical Engineering	540	324	216	40.00
Computer Science and Engineering	6400	3520	2880	45.00
Information Technology	2700	1620	1080	40.00
Electronics and Communication Engineering	6625	4625	2000	30.20
Electrical Engineering	3600	1980	1620	45.00
Polymer Engineering	240	120	120	50.00
Production cum Plant Engineering	240	192	48	20.00
Applied Electronics and Instrumentation Engineering	720	648	72	10.00
Electronics and Instrumentation	495	250	245	57.10
Architecture	320	165	155	48.43
Bio Medical Engineering	320	132	188	58.70
Industrial Engineering	120	90	30	25.00
Instrumentation and Control Engineering	240	195	45	18.75
Mechanical Engineering	3964	3924	40	1.00
Mechanical Engineering (Production)	240	228	12	5.00
Total	29172	19263	9909	33.96

Source: Directorate of Technical Education, Trivandrum

wise intake in government ITIs and private ITCs (one year course) shows the predominance of girls in stenography, dress making, cutting and tailoring, secretarial practice and data preparation (Eapen and Kodoth 2004).

This comparative analysis of enrolment in various courses indicates that there is a large number of females in the general arts and science courses at graduate and postgraduate levels. One possible reason could be that the rise in the female mean age at marriage is forcing them to continue education till they find a suitable alliance. Even in the marriage market, men seem to prefer equally educated or even higher educated girls as brides,[12] pushing up the enrolment of girls

[12]There is a trend among the less educated men who emigrate, to marry relatively better educated women (Zachariah et al. 2003).

in higher education. However similar trends are not visible in the enrolment pattern of professional courses in technical schools, polytechnics and engineering colleges. The important exceptions are nursing and teaching, professions traditionally closely identified with women and thus having only a small male presence (Kodoth and Eapen 2005). On the whole it appears that women's education has not played the transformative role generally expected of it; on the contrary it seems to have furthered conformity to gender roles.

Work Participation and Unemployment

The previous analysis has shown that women in Kerala have high levels of educational attainment not found anywhere else in the country. Hence, given the general hypothesis that education increases female labour force participation, it is normal to expect a healthy work participation rate among them. However, contrary to expectations, Kerala experiences the lowest female work participation rate (Eapen 1992; Kumar 1992; Gulati and Rajan 1997; Kodoth and Eapen 2005) and highest unemployment among the major states in India. As per the 1991 and 2001 Census Kerala ranks twenty-second and thirty-second respectively among all the regions (including states and union territories) in terms of female work participation rate.[13] Table 2.6 presents the census estimates of work participation rates by sex in Kerala during 1901–2001. It can be seen from the table that though the work participation rates of both males and females have declined over the said period, the decline has been sharpest for female work participation with a fall of 52.3 percentage points as against only 5.9 percentage points for males. Meanwhile from 1981 onwards there has been a consistent increase in the work participation rate of males with a simultaneous decline in female work participation rate, except urban female work participation which showed improvement, resulting in a widening gender gap in work force participation which was at its peak at 35.7% in 2001.

The picture at the national level is quite the opposite with an increase in the female work participation (14.2 to 25.6%) and a decline in male work participation (52.8 to 51.8%) during the period 1971–2001. The gender gap in the work participation rate at the national level, therefore, has narrowed down from 38.6% in 1971 to

[13]As per Census definitions, work participation rate is defined as the percentage of total workers in total population.

Table 2.6 Work Participation Rates in Kerala by Sex, 1901–2001

Year	*Male*	*Female*	*Gap*
1901	56.3	32.7	23.6
1911	53.8	28.9	24.9
1921	51.1	24.5	26.6
1931	50.0	35.9	14.1
1941	NA	NA	NA
1951	46.7	18.3	28.4
1961	47.2	19.7	27.5
1971	45.2	14.6	30.6
1981	44.9	16.6	28.3
1991	47.6	15.9	31.7
2001	50.4	15.3	35.7

Source: Compiled by the authors from various Census reports

26.2% in 2001. The statistics reveal that despite a favourable educational environment for women in Kerala, the state exhibits a regressive trend in female work participation as compared to the all India level.

Table 2.7 shows the distribution of workers in primary and non-primary sectors of Kerala during 1961 to 2001. The proportion of males and females employed in the primary sector has recorded a decline in rural and urban areas whereas it has increased in the non-primary sector. The work participation rate of both males and females of rural areas has shown a consistent decline since 1971. In female work participation, the largest change between primary and non-primary sectors has taken place during the last decade. For instance, in rural areas, female work participation rate recorded a decline of 38% in the primary sector whereas it increased by 40.9% in the non-primary sector. In urban areas, the female work participation declined by 55.25% in the primary sector and increased 15.45% in the non-primary sector.

The National Sample Survey Organization (NSSO) conducts nation-wide surveys at regular intervals to assess the labour force participation of the population by gender and place of residence (NSSO 1990; 1996; 2001). Table 2.8 presents the trends and patterns of female work participation rates for Kerala and India. Using the NSSO data which adopts a more extended definition of work, we find that women in Kerala have a low work participation rate both

Table 2.7 Work Participation Rate in Primary and Non-Primary Sectors by Sex and Residence in Kerala, 1961–2001

Year	*Primary*		*Non-primary*	
	Males	*Females*	*Males*	*Females*
Rural				
1961	41.1	46.9	58.9	53.1
1971	53.4	58.2	46.6	41.8
1981	47.1	55.6	52.9	44.4
1991	35.5	51.6	64.5	48.4
2001	27.6	31.8	72.4	68.2
Urban				
1961	7.2	15.4	92.8	84.6
1971	8.9	20.2	91.1	79.8
1981	10.5	18.2	89.5	81.8
1991	11.9	21.9	88.1	78.1
2001	6.7	9.8	93.3	90.2

Source: Compiled by the authors from various Census reports

Note: Cultivators and agricultural labourers included among Primary sectors and others

Table 2.8 Workforce Participation Rates by Sex and Residence, 1987–88 to 1999–2000

	Kerala			*India*		
	43rd round (1987–88)	*50th round (1993–94)*	*55th round (1999–2000)*	*43rd round (1987–88)*	*50th round (1993–94)*	*55th round (1999–2000)*
Total						
Persons	38.6	38.3	38.7	41.1	41.8	39.5
Males	51.2	54.3	55.4	53.1	54.4	52.7
Females	26.5	22.9	22.9	28.1	28.3	25.4
Rural						
Males	50.6	53.7	55.3	53.9	55.3	53.1
Females	28.6	23.8	23.8	32.6	32.8	29.9
Urban						
Males	53.0	55.9	55.8	50.6	52.1	51.8
Females	19.8	20.3	20.3	15.2	15.5	13.9

Source: NSSO (1990), (1996), (2001)

Note: Work participation rates are in percentages and measured by usual principal and subsidiary status

in relation to women at the national level and men in the state. At the national level the female work participation rate was 25.4% as against 22.9% in Kerala. The state had a lower proportion of rural females and a higher proportion of urban females in the workforce compared to the national level. During 1987–8 and 1993–4, the female work participation rate recorded a considerable decline of 4.8 percentage points in Kerala. The sex ratio of the work force reveals that the number of female workers per 1000 male workers has declined from 536 in 1987–8 to 436 in 1999–2000 (NSSO 1990, 1996, 2001). This clearly reflects the declining trend of female workforce participation in Kerala.

While discussing the declining female work participation rates, studies have pointed out that it could be due to multiplicity of causes. The recession experienced in the Kerala economy during the second half of the 1990s has been a major factor contributing to the stagnation in the work participation rates.[14] Moreover economic marginalization, gender discrimination in the labour market, occupational sex-segregation and the falling demand for female labour, technological obsolescence, mismatch between labour demand and supply have been cited as reasons for low levels of work participation among females. Other reasons include lack of fresh investments in the state, changing expectations of job, and a faulty educational system. (Eapen 1992; Kumar 1994; Mathew 1995; Government of Kerala 2003). Another line of argument is that, bolstered by higher male work participation rates, higher wages and household earnings, women are withdrawing into full time domestic activities. This could reflect an informed choice, an option reflecting greater leisure or time to attend to household or family concerns (Kodoth and Eapen 2005:3281). One of the major consequences of declining female work participation rate, however, is that it entails a considerable risk by reducing women's access to earned incomes and therefore, increases their dependant status (Kodoth and Eapen 2005:3281).

The low female work participation rate could also be attributed to the fact that after education, women have withdrawn from manual labour, but have not yet obtained other kinds of jobs according to their changed preference and expectation (Government of Kerala 2004: 31). This argument is again supported by a recent study on women's employment preference highlighting the fact that nearly

[14]See Prakash et al. 2004 for greater discussion on the reasons for low work participation rate in rural Kerala.

three-fourth of the women in central Kerala reported to be unemployed on account of inability to find jobs as per their preference. Of the factors mediating preference, social status and proximity to home were some of the most important criterions (Lakshmi 2002).

Studies have also shown that the low female work participation rates in Kerala indicate the existence of large proportion of unemployed women in the labour force (Eapen 2004). According to the estimates by Economics and Statistics Department, nearly 60% of the female labour force in the state remains unemployed (Moli 2004: 63). Further, among 40.05 lakh job seekers registered with employment exchanges in the state in 2003, 23.10 lakh are females and 16.95 lakh are male job seekers. Notably, Kerala's peculiar feature of the unemployment scenario is that women outnumber men in seeking employment through employment exchanges in all the fourteen districts of the state. The estimates by National Sample Survey for Kerala show a higher female unemployment rate of 26% as compared to 20% for males in the rural sector. In the urban areas this proportion is about 28% and 15% respectively (NSSO 2001). The problem is more severe among the educated females of the state with almost a quarter of women graduates in rural areas being unable to procure employment as compared to 13% of men (Eapen and Kodoth 2004). In Kerala, female educated unemployment in urban areas is 34.2% compared to 36.7% in rural areas in 1999–2000. On the other hand, the female educated unemployment in urban and rural areas of India is 14.3% and 14.6% respectively for the same period. Moreover while the educated unemployment rate among males (rural and urban) has declined, the same has increased for women between fiftieth and fifty-fifth rounds of national sample survey (Table 2.9).

An estimation based on the Kerala migration survey indicates that the unemployment rate was 11.2% among males and about 41.2% or four times higher among females in 2003. It also points out that females contributed to two-thirds of the increase in unemployment in Kerala during 1998–2003, indicating a noteworthy development in the unemployment scenario of the state (Zachariah and Rajan 2005). It follows that education alone does not enable women to acquire gender equity in economic participation; rather it is a combination of individual and household characteristics, which mediate such decisions for women (Sebastian 2005).

Labour force participation not only gives women an opportunity to earn an income, but also exposes them to the outside world and to authority structures and networks other than kin-based ones (Dixon

Table 2.9 Educated Unemployment Rates in Kerala, 1993–94 to 1999–2000

Category of Workers	*Kerala*		*India*	
	50th round (1993–94)	*55th round (1999–2000)*	*50th round (1993–94)*	*55th round (1999–2000)*
Usual principal and subsidiary status (UPSS)				
Rural male	15.6	11.2	6.5	5.6
Rural female	32.3	36.7	15.0	14.6
Urban male	11.2	7.4	6.0	6.2
Urban female	34.9	34.2	18.2	14.3
Usual principal status (UPS)				
Rural male	18.5	15.0	8.8	6.8
Rural female	49.6	49.1	24.9	20.4
Urban male	12.6	9.9	6.9	6.6
Urban female	40.6	41.9	20.6	16.3

Source: NSSO (1996), (2001)
Note: Work participation rates are in percentages

and Mueller 1993). Further, it is generally expected that women who work at regular jobs, perceive that their contribution plays a substantial part in the total family income and are therefore, more empowered than temporarily employed or unemployed women (Youssef 1982; Sen 1990; Mahmud and Johnston 1994). Moreover participation of women in economic activities outside the home has been shown to have an important bearing on gender relations within the household. Dwyer and Bruce (1988) and Blumberg (1991) point out that the main factor that affects intra-household gender relations is the relative incomes of males and females. Women's economic power, defined as the control of key economic resources such as income, property, and other means of production relative to that of men is posited as the most important dependent variable affecting gender relations at the household level. Changing levels of female employment, however, along with the persistence of a gendered work structure have limited women's claims to 'self-acquired' or independent sources of wealth in Kerala (Eapen and Kodoth 2004).

This line of argument might explain the poor performance of the state in non-conventional gender empowerment indicators, which capture power and autonomy. The role of women in decision-making activities is supposed to be a good measure to assess their empowerment. At the national level, 9.4% of women do not get involved in any decision-making compared to 7.2% of women in Kerala. However, the percentage of women excluded from decision-making is much higher in Kerala as compared to many other states like Gujarat, Haryana, Punjab and Tamil Nadu. In Kerala, 48% of the women do not need permission to go to the market whereas 38% do not need permission to visit friends or relatives. This proportion is 32% and 24% respectively at the national level. Though the figures are above the national average, they are lower than those of Tamil Nadu, Gujarat and Punjab (IIPS 2000), which are states with much lower levels of female educational attainments. It is argued that high educational status indicates better status of women but Kerala's experience indicates that neither female literacy nor higher education are sufficient conditions for women's empowerment.

Demographic Transition and Life Expectancy

Kerala's performance in terms of improvement in mortality indicators has been outstanding over the last five decades. Kerala consistently had a lower level of mortality than that of India as a whole even during 1951–61. The Crude Death Rate of Kerala declined from 19.7 (per 1000 population) in 1951–61 to 12.2 in 1961–71 (Rajan and Zachariah 1998) and has reached 6.4 in 2002 (as per SRS estimates). It would appear that people in Kerala have, all along, enjoyed a better and healthier life than people in other parts of the country (Rajan, Bhat and Dyson 1997). The mortality outcome of Kerala is on account of many interrelated factors such as growth of education and the resultant cleanliness, availability of safe drinking water and good sanitation facilities, better nutrition, health care provision through different stream of medicines both modern and traditional, and health infrastructure. As a result of this, as pointed out earlier, almost all the health indicators in the state become comparable with that of developed countries.

Life expectancy is again one of the important health indicators, which has shown a remarkable improvement in Kerala among both males and females. Between 1911 and 1960, the expectation of life had increased by 21 years for males and 23 years for females (Rajan and Zachariah 1998). Today a man and a woman in Kerala are expected to live close to 71 and 76 years respectively (Table 2.10) which is approximately 10 to 13 years longer than the average life expectancy

Table 2.10 Estimates of Life Expectancy for Kerala and India, 1970–75 to 1997–2001 (in years)

Year	*Kerala*				*India*			
	Total	*Male*	*Female*	*Female–male gap (in years)*	*Total*	*Male*	*Female*	*Female-male gap (in years)*
1970–75	62.0	60.8	63.3	2.5	49.7	50.5	49.0	-1.5
1976–80	65.5	63.5	67.6	4.1	52.3	52.5	52.1	-0.4
1981–85	68.4	65.4	71.5	6.1	55.5	55.4	55.7	0.3
1986–90	69.5	66.8	72.3	5.5	57.7	57.7	58.1	0.4
1991–95	72.9	69.9	73.3	3.4	60.3	59.7	60.9	1.2
1992–96	73.1	70.2	75.8	5.6	60.7	60.1	61.4	1.3
1993–97	73.3	70.4	75.9	5.5	61.1	60.4	61.8	1.4
1994–98	73.4	70.5	76.0	5.5	61.4	60.6	62.2	1.6
1995–99	73.5	70.6	76.1	5.5	61.7	60.8	62.5	1.7
1999–2000	73.5	70.7	76.1	5.4	61.9	61.0	62.7	1.7
2000–2001	73.6	70.8	76.2	5.4	62.2	61.3	63.0	1.7

Source: Compiled by the authors from Sample Registration System

of men and women in India as a whole. Although life expectancy at birth has improved for both Kerala and India as a whole, in India, female life expectancy has only moderately overtaken male life expectancy as compared to the five-year plus advantage for women in Kerala as per 2001 census estimates.[15] In a nutshell, women today in Kerala live 13 years longer than women in other parts of the country. Moreover they also live more than five years longer than their male counterparts. But it may not all be an unqualified gain for Kerala as it brings challenges of another kind related to aging and high incidence of widowhood among women (Gulati 1993; Sreerupa 2006).

EMERGENT CRISES IN GENDER PARITY: SOME ISSUES

In the previous section we discussed some aspects of gender disparity in the social development of contemporary Kerala. Now we move on to exploring the future crises in gender parity with respect to certain emergent issues in the Kerala society such as aging, migration,

[15]Elsewhere in the world, women generally experience lower mortality than men at almost all ages such that the life expectancy at birth of women is greater by 5 to 8 years compared to that of men (Visaria 2002).

changing juvenile sex ratio and rising crime rates. Societal aging, a fallout of the decline in fertility and mortality, is turning out to be a women's issue with women living longer and constituting the bulk of the very old population. Another notable demographic phenomenon of Kerala is migration and the fact that opportunities and enabling influences associated with it are not as easily accessible to the women in the state as they are to the men. Meanwhile a female dominated population sex ratio, seen as the most illustrative summary measure of the historical status of women in Kerala, masks a falling juvenile sex ratio. Another disturbing trend is the rising rate of crime against women including domestic violence.

Aging and Women

Kerala is the only state in India that is at an advanced stage of demographic transition.[16] The combination of high fertility and falling mortality during the twentieth century has ensured large and rapid increases in the elderly population as successively larger numbers enter old age. Accompanied by the sharp recent decline in fertility, it has led to an even greater proportion of elderly in the population (Rajan et al. 1999, 2003a). The state has 10.4% elderly, the highest proportion amongst states, compared to 7.4% at the national level in 2001.

A notable demographic feature of the Kerala population is the 'feminization of aging', an increase in the share of the women among the older population. The favourable female-male ratio and high female life expectancy at birth in Kerala has contributed to the growing proportion of female elderly in the population. It can be observed from Figure 2.2 that the elderly sex ratio is exceptionally favourable to females especially, those of age 70 years and above.

In Kerala, women not only outnumber men but also outlive them as shown in the previous section. As of now, at age 60, a Malayali woman is expected to live 20.61 years as against 18.08 years by her male counterpart. Similarly, at age 70, a woman's life expectancy is 13.31 years and a man's, 12.62 years. Factors such as the higher female life expectancy at ages 60 and 70, the universal tendency for women to marry men older than themselves and the social restrictions on widows to remarry, lead to a high incidence of widowhood among

[16] It is a process involving shift from high fertility and high mortality regime to low or declining fertility and low mortality.

Figure 2.2 Trends in Sex Ratio among Elderly (60-plus) in Kerala, 1961–2026

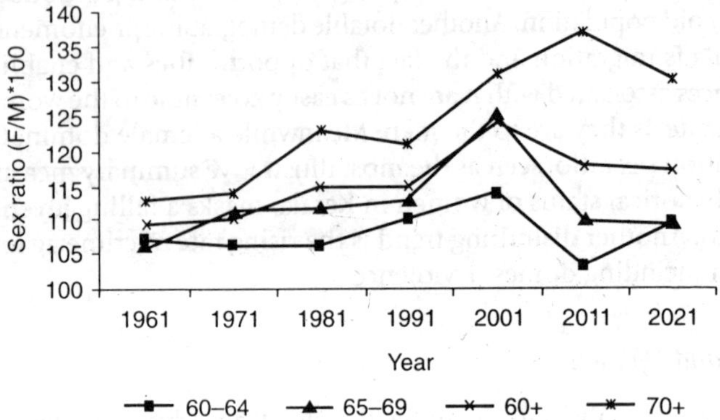

Source: Rajan et al. (1999)
Note: Sex ratio for the year 2011 and 2021 are estimated from projected population

Figure 2.3 Incidence of Widowhood in Kerala and India among 60-plus Male and Female

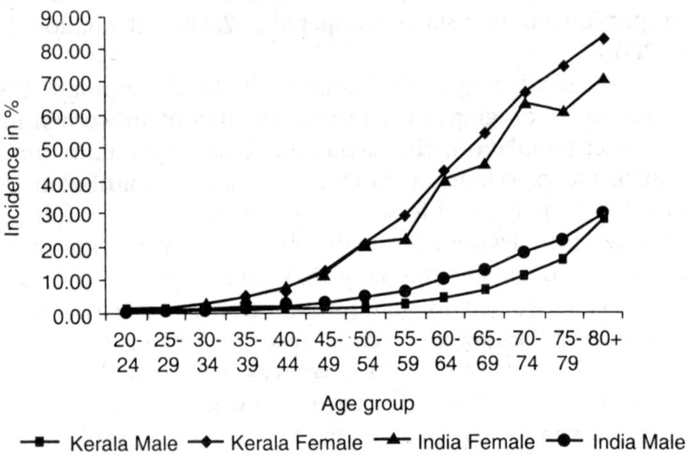

Source: Computed by the authors based on the Census data

the female elderly (Gulati and Irudaya Rajan 1997). The incidence of widowhood among elderly women is greater in Kerala as compared to India as a whole (Figure 2.3).

The gender gap in the incidence of female widowhood is about six times more in Kerala compared to only slightly more than three times at the national level. 83% of women widowed, as against 28% of men are among the oldest–old, or those aged 80 years and above. In other words, in the 80-plus age group, 3 out of every 10 elderly men and 8 out of 10 elderly women are widowed in both rural and urban areas. The corresponding figures at the national level are 71% and 29% respectively as seen in Figure 2.3. It can be seen that at any given age, there are more widows than widowers and as age advances, the prevalence of widowhood also increases.

Longevity though a remarkable developmental achievement, puts elderly women in a unique position where they occupy two stigmatized statuses, being female and old. The negative effects of both combine to make older women a particularly disadvantaged group who are, hence, in double jeopardy (Chappell and Havens 1980). To add to this, when old age is dovetailed with widowhood, the women face severe socio-economic disadvantages and health vulnerability (Sreerupa 2006). Undoubtedly women enjoy added years, but as the following discussion reveals, the accumulated disadvantages suffered by them over their life course compromises their quality of life in the later years.

One of the associated hazards of old age is the decline in income and financial dependency, exacerbated for the elderly women, due to their life time involvement in unpaid domestic work or low paid work. Since women have historically lagged behind men in getting regular employment they also miss out on pension and other benefits (Prasad 2005). The trend of very low female work participation in Kerala continues even among the aged with most of the elderly women reporting to be non-workers as per census 2001. The financial inadequacy seems to be of a higher degree for the female elderly compared to the male elderly (Dak and Sharma 1987; Nandal et al. 1987). According to the NSS fifty-second round data on the elderly, more than 75% of aged women in Kerala do not own any financial assets, whereas close to 54% do not own any property as compared to 58% and 52% respectively of the aged women in India (Rajan 2006).

Most of the elderly will depend on their children for financial support in the absence of extra-familial, state or institutional support for the elderly. The adverse marital status, however, could influence the overall level of care and support received by them from their family as well as society at large. It is assumed that the living arrangements of the elderly play an important role in their socio-economic security. However, it is possible that co-residence may not ensure healthy relationship between generations, and economic, social and emotional support may be provided by the younger generation, even without co-residence. Table 2.11 shows the different types of living arrangements. Co-residence with children and grand children is supposed to be the best living arrangement for elderly as it ensures a greater level of well-being for them (Rajan and Kumar 2003:75).

A recent study undertaken by the Centre for Development Studies[17] shows that 2.5% (4% females and less than 1% males) of the elderly live alone. The majority of the elderly living alone are widows. The number of male elderly persons living with spouse is twice the number of female elderly in the same category. More elderly females than elderly males live without spouse but with children, grand children or other relatives due to the high incidence of widowhood among the elderly females. Elderly people living in a household with non-relatives is not very common in Kerala (Table 2.11).

Table 2.11 Living Arrangements of Elderly in Kerala, 2004

Living Arrangements	*Male*	*Female*	*Total*
Living alone	0.95	3.94	2.54
Living with spouse	10.56	5.07	7.65
With spouse, children and grand children	76.11	50.51	62.54
Without spouse but with children, grand children	11.42	38.47	25.76
Without spouse, but with relatives other than children and grand children	0.79	1.87	1.36
With non relatives	0.17	0.15	0.16
Total	100	100	100

Source: Rajan and Aliyar (2004)

Another important dimension of the living arrangement of the elderly is old age homes. The total number of old age homes in Kerala is about 200, which is one-fifth of all the old age homes in the country (Rajan 2002, 2006). Currently at least five old age homes are coming up every year. The number of female elderly inmates in old age homes in Kerala is about 64% (Rajan and Aliyar 2004:80). It is important

[17]The Kerala Aging Survey (2005) was conducted by Centre for Development Studies among more than 5,012 elderly in 14 districts, covering 225 panchayats and coordinated by the senior author of this paper. This study was financed by the Indo-Dutch Program on Alternatives in Development and Shastri Indo-Canadian Institute.

to note the increasing proportion of female elderly either staying alone or being institutionalized in Kerala. It clearly indicates that societal aging is turning out to be a women's problem. Future programmes and policy perspectives related to the elderly, have, therefore, to be made gender sensitive.

Migration

Migration is not only a remarkable demographic phenomenon but also one having far reaching significance for the economic and social fabric of the state. Kerala has experienced large scale out migration over the years especially since the oil boom and the resultant increase in economic activities in Gulf region attracted a large number of Malayali emigrants[18] to these countries in the early 1970s. The majority of such emigrants were unskilled or semi-skilled male workers who were engaged in construction related works. There were about 1.8 million emigrants from Kerala in 2004, 1.5 million males and 0.3 million females, the females constituting only about 16% of the total emigrants (Zachariah and Rajan 2004). This signifies that the opportunities opened up by the possibility of emigration are not equally available to men and women. A look at the marital status-wise break up of the female emigrant population shows that only 25% of them are unmarried as against 61% males, which raises the question whether a majority of the female emigrants are those accompanying their spouses rather than going for employment.

A comprehensive survey undertaken by Centre for Development Studies, entitled Kerala Migration Survey (1998–9) collected information on various dimensions of migration from Kerala covering 10,000 households at random from all the districts and *taluks* in the state. This survey indicates that women constitute 9.6% of the total migrants from the state. In the case of emigration or return emigration, one out of every ten migrant was a woman in 1998 (Zachariah et al. 2003:311). Females constitute 24% of outward migrants and 29% of return out migrants. 10% of the emigrants are females with the highest concentration from Thrissur district while Malappuram district has the largest number of male emigrants.

Between 1983–7 and 1993–7, female out migration recorded a fast growth compared to female emigration which was sluggish. For

[18]The migration from Kerala was so large that they are often referred to as the 'Malayalee Diaspora'.

instance, female emigrants increased by 2.5 times and male emigrants, 4 times. On the other hand, the number of female out migrants grew by 6.9 times while that of male out migrants rose by 3.3 times during the aforesaid period. Females constitute 11% of total return emigrants and 29.2% of total return out migrants.

Apart from the low level of migration amongst women it would be worth exploring how much difference this migration status brings to their level of economic activity. The level of economic activity has been assessed at the place of origin before migration, at the destination, and after returning to the place of origin (Table 2.12). Among those who emigrated, about 98% of the males and 53% of the females were engaged in various economic activities at the place of origin. After emigration, (at destination) the female economic activity rose slightly to 57% and later experienced a sharp decline to 21% once they came back. At the place of origin, the gender differential in economic activity among emigrants was 45.3% before emigration, increasing to 76.3% after their return.

Table 2.12 Economic Activity Rates by Migration Status (percentages)

	Emigrants			*Out migrants*		
	M	*F*	*Difference*	*M*	*F*	*Difference*
At the origin	98.4	53.1	45.3	86.9	55.6	31.3
At the destination	98.9	57.3	41.6	93.4	56.9	36.5
After return	97.6	21.3	76.3	93.4	28.6	64.8

Source: Zachariah et al. (2003)

Male out migrants have a high participation in economic activity at the place of destination as well as origin once they return, compared to their participation rates at the place of origin before migration. Female out migration did not improve the economic activity rates much, but showed a decline after their return. In a nutshell, though both emigration and out migration tend to slightly increase the economic activity rates of females; their return to the place of origin significantly reduces their economic participation rates.

A most significant social impact of migration is the effect it has on the family of the migrant. Migration has a notable effect on the married women who are separated from their husbands. It was estimated that husbands of about 13% of married women in Kerala work away from Kerala. In terms of absolute numbers, it comes to about 981,000 married women (Zachariah et al. 2003). The most important adverse effects of this phenomenon is on the women left behind who experience loneliness, added responsibilities in the absence of their husbands and indebtedness due to loans raised at the time of migration (specifically emigration).

The impact on women left behind at home may also be positive depending on the level of autonomy enjoyed by them and the exercise of their agency. An important positive impact could be the changes occurring in life standard and consumption pattern of a household with a migrant. Also, women get more exposure to the outside world on a day-to-day basis. They start handling large amounts of money and engage in various activities outside the house like opening accounts in banks, going to different offices, hospitals and doing other work in the absence of their husbands. Most of these activities were unfamiliar to them before the migration of their husbands, specifically emigration.

Changing Juvenile Sex Ratio

Ramachandran (1996) has reported that sex ratio is perhaps the most illustrative summary measure of the historical status of women in Kerala. Indeed, Kerala stands out as a positive example in a country with an exceptionally low female-male ratio. We should not lose sight of the fact that what Kerala is experiencing is merely a 'normal' female-dominant population sex ratio (Rajan and Sudha 2000) indicating a lack of female disadvantage in survival unlike in other parts of the country.

Meanwhile, recent studies, using evidence from a variety of sources, have shown that female survival disadvantage has persisted, if not increased, in India during the phase of economic development and fertility-mortality decline (Das Gupta and Bhat 1997; Basu 1999; Rajan and Sudha 2000). This is reflected in the increased masculinity of sex ratios at birth and persistent excess female child mortality. This trend is contrary to available evidence to the effect that, even though males outnumber females at birth, given similar care, women tend to have lower age-specific mortality rate than men (Dreze and Sen 1995). Hence all these studies conclude that the male bias seems to be intensifying; moreover they add that the trend seems to be spreading to South India as well. However the question remains whether Kerala is still an exception.

We start exploring the situation by examining the juvenile sex ratio i.e. the sex ratio among children between the ages of 0 and 6 years in Kerala. The juvenile sex ratio has shown fluctuations since 1961, when it was 972 per 1000 males, to 1971, when it increased slightly to 976 per 1000 males. It has been on a downward trend since, falling to 970, and further to 958, in 1981 and 1991 respectively. Since 1971, it was only in 2001 that the juvenile sex ratio showed a slight improvement of two points. The falling juvenile sex ratio in Kerala must be noted as a warning sign of the spread of female disadvantage in survival, though the sex ratio is still well above the national average.

A comparison of juvenile sex ratio in 61 *taluks* of Kerala based on the 1991 and 2001 census indicates that, in more than 34 *taluks*, it has shown an increasing trend. In 25 *taluks*, it has declined and in two *taluks*, it has been constant. *Taluks* such as Aluva, Kannur, Kollam, Manathavady, Peermade, Sulthanbathery and Thiruvanathapuram have recorded a decline of more than 10 points in juvenile sex ratio in 2001 compared to 1991. Among urban *taluks*, Pathanampuram with 911 has the highest, and in rural *taluks*, Kuttanad and Aluva with 945 have the lowest child sex ratio. Though none of the districts or *taluks* in the state experience an extreme scenario like that of Punjab, Haryana or Rajasthan, the declining juvenile sex ratio seems to be an indication of either excess female child mortality, postnatal discrimination or sex selective abortion, prenatal discrimination, or some combination of the two.

The SRS reports the infant mortality rate (IMR) of Kerala as 10 in 2003, while the rest of India lags behind in the position where Kerala stood in the late 1960s. As of 2003, the IMR stood at 12 for rural areas and 10 for urban areas of Kerala. Notably in urban areas, IMR was estimated to be 8 for males and 12 for females (Registrar General 2005), that is, the female death rate is greater than that of male. This could be an indication of postnatal discrimination. It appears that female children in Kerala may have begun to experience mortality disadvantage, that was non-existent earlier.

The declining juvenile sex ratio and its correlation with increasing ultra sound scanning centres needs special attention. There were only about 100 ultra sound centres in the state a decade ago, a number which rose to 850 in 2004 (Soma Wadhwa 2004). The growth of such facilities may suggest a growing demand for sex determination of the foetus and possibility of sex selective abortions, though further research is needed to establish a conclusive relation between the two trends. Meanwhile a recent study at Achuta Menon Centre for Health Sciences has estimated that about 30,000 female foeticides occur in Kerala annually. Further an anthropological study on this subject conducted in Trichur, reports evidence of female foeticide in Kerala (Sudha et al. forthcoming).

Rising Crime Rates

Besides the above-discussed issues, certain disturbing trends in the Kerala society reveal the changing attitude towards women. According to the estimates of the National Crime Records Bureau, the crime rates in Kerala have risen four-fold during 1991–7, of which rape and domestic violence are reported to be the highest. Kerala ranks first among the states in overall crimes against women, particularly molestation and cruelty at home. According to the estimates by the National Crime Records Bureau, there has been an increase in home cruelty rates, molestation, and sexual harassment during 1995–2000. Kerala's higher ranking could be due to better reporting. In other states, due to illiteracy, ignorance, muscle and political power, crimes against women would be under-reported. Nevertheless, these trends are an eye opener to a society which is still basking in the glory of its socio-cultural wealth of the high status of women in the society.

Today both macro and micro level evidence is available to assess the pattern and magnitude of violence against women in Kerala. It is important to note that, Kerala had a higher proportion of women reporting violence at least once in their lifetime, (70.2%) than the all India level (IIPS 2000). Disappointingly, 60.8% of women in Kerala justified wife beating on one or other grounds, as against only 53% for all India. It is unfortunate that mass female literacy and high levels of educational attainments among the women in the state cannot dissuade them from rationalizing domestic violence. Literacy and better education are considered important means by which knowledge and information are acquired and a progressive attitude towards gender equality ingrained. However, high female education in Kerala, rather than contributing to the emancipation of women, has led to social conformity and dependence (Saradamoni 1994, 1999).

A study carried out in seven cities in India on domestic violence found out that violence by husbands is fairly widespread. Among the cities, Trivandrum had the highest prevalence of overall violence during 1997–9. Women in Trivandrum are reported to experience levels of physical violence similar to women in Vellore and Lucknow

(International Clinical Epidemiology Network 2000). In a study of 133 survivors who attempted suicide between 1994–5, more than half of them were women. 48% of women, 36 out of 75 reported marital disharmony as the prime cause of suicide attempts. Also, one third of these women had suffered domestic violence (Jayasree 1997). There are clear indications that violence and mental distress are growing to be a serious problem in Kerala, warranting social concern and intervention (Mohammed et al. 2002; Eapen and Kodoth 2004).

CONCLUDING OBSERVATIONS

Kerala has been the champion of health and demographic transition in the country. The 'Kerala development model' has been hailed for its remarkable achievements of high literacy, low fertility, and good health indicators comparable with some of the developed nations. The outstanding gains made by women with respect to some of these conventional indicators were seen as evidence for gender parity in the society. However recent studies have shown that Kerala scores poorly in terms of non-conventional indicators attempting to capture power and subordination of women. The deteriorating status of women in Kerala society seems to be reflected in the low female work participation, high unemployment, dwindling juvenile sex ratio, rising crime against women among others.

In terms of overall literacy and enrolment until high school level, the state has almost wiped out the gender disparities. The gender bias or disadvantage is noticed, however, in the choice of courses for higher education, where women seem to be shying away from professional and technical education, raising questions about the role of family and society at large in mediating and influencing their choice of education and occupation. Another area of concern is the declining female work participation and the increasing number of unemployed females in the state. The declining female work participation in comparison to male work participation results in a widening gender gap which entails a considerable risk of reducing women's access to earned income thus, increasing their dependent status.

At the same time, Kerala society is also facing emergent challenges such as a growing elderly population, unemployment, migration, changing juvenile sex ratio and rising crime against women which have a distinct gender concern attached with them. It is, therefore, important to ensure that all policy initiatives take these into consideration. It was found that though the overall sex ratio was favourable to females, the juvenile sex ratio was turning unfavourable to them. The low juvenile sex ratio and the growing number of ultra sound scan centres in the state seem to suggest a trend towards female child survival disadvantage, much like that found in North India. Further research is needed to explore the link between declining juvenile sex ratio and the growth of ultra sound scan centres in the state which could pose a challenge for policy makers in future. Further, the growing number of female elderly, specifically widows, needs special attention especially with regard to their economic and health security. All future policies and programmes for the elderly, therefore, have to be made gender sensitive. Lastly the rising trend of crime against women is one of the gravest challenges for the well being of women in Kerala. In a nutshell, given the overall scenario of declining women's status in the state, there is no scope for complacency on this score on the part of the civil society, policy makers and academia.

APPENDIX

Table A2.1: Percentage of Girls Enrolment to Total Enrolment by Stages in India, 1950–51 to 2003

Year	*Primary (I–V)*	*Middle (VI–VIII)*	*Sec./Hr. Sec/ 10+2/In Sec./ Hr. Sec/ 10+2/Inter*	*Higher education (Degree & above level)*
1950–51	28.1	16.1	13.3	10.0
1960–61	32.6	23.9	20.5	16.0
1970–71	37.4	29.3	25.0	20.0
1980–81	38.6	32.9	29.6	26.7
1990–91	41.5	36.7	32.9	33.3
2000–01*	43.7	40.9	38.6	39.4
2002–03*	46.8	43.9	41.3	40.1

Source: Government of India (2002)
Note: * Indicates provisional estimates

Table A2.2: Sex-wise Distribution of Enrolment in HSS, VHSC, ICSE and CBSE schools

Type of Schools	*Boys*	*Girls*	*Total students*
Higher secondary schools*	144961 (42.7)	194392 (57.3)	339353
Vocational higher secondary*	26076 (46.7)	29821 (53.3)	55893
Kendriya Vidyalaya**	17104 (54.2)	14471 (45.8)	31575
Navodaya**	3477 (58.4)	2483 (41.6)	5962
CBSE**	125406 (55.8)	99179 (44.2)	224585
ICSE**	26927 (58.4)	19160 (41.6)	46087

Source: Directorate of Public Instruction, Trivandrum
Note: *Indicates estimates for 2002–3
** Indicates estimates for 2001–2. Figures in the parenthesis are percentage distributions

Table A2.3: Sex-wise Distribution of Enrolment in Degree and Post-graduate Level in Kerala, 1999–2004 (in 000s)

Year	*Degree*			*Post-graduate*		
	M	*F*	*Percentage of females*	*M*	*F*	*Percentage of females*
1999	48	83	63.4	3	9	75.0
2000	52	93	64.1	4	11	73.3
2001	NA	NA	NA	NA	NA	NA
2002	56	89	61.4	5	10	66.6
2003	55	88	61.1	5	10	66.6
2004	54	99	64.7	4	12	75.0

Source: Directorate of Collegiate Education

Table A2.4: Number of Students Appeared and Passed in Entrance Examinations, 2004

Courses	*Male*			*Female*			*Percentage of females to total appeared*
	Appeared	*Qualified*	*%*	*Appeared*	*Qualified*	*%*	
Engineering	27173	20119	74.0	21251	15318	72.1	43.86
Medical	18612	16369	87.9	29128	25361	87.1	61.01

Source: Commissionerate of Entrance Examination, Trivandrum

REFERENCES

Achin, Chakraborty, 2005, 'Kerala's Changing Development Narratives', *Economic and Political Weekly*, Vol. 40, No. 6, pp. 541–54.

Ambili, C.S., 1999, 'Growth of School Education in Kerala: Pattern and Differentials', unpublished M.Phil. Dissertation, Trivandrum: Centre for Development Studies.

Basu, A.M., 1999, 'Fertility Decline and Increasing Gender Imbalance In India, Including a Possible South Indian Turnaround', *Development and Change*, 30 (2) pp. 237–63.

Bhat, P.N and Rajan, S.I., 1990, 'Demographic Transition in Kerala Revisited', *Economic and Political Weekly*, Vol. 25, Nos. 35 and 36, pp. 1957–80.

Blumberg, Rae Lesser, 1991, (ed.), *Gender, Family and Economy: The Triple Overlap*, California: Sage Publications.

Chappell, Neena and Havens, Betty, 1980, 'Old and Female: Testing the Double Jeopardy Hypothesis', *Sociological Quarterly*, 21, pp. 157–71.

Dak, T.M. and Sharma, M.L., 1987, 'Changing Status of the Aged in the North Indian Villages', T.M. Dak and M.L. Sharma (eds.), *Aging in India*, New Delhi: Ajanta Publications, pp. 43–55.

Das Gupta, M. and Bhat, P.N., 1997, 'Fertility Decline and Increased Manifestation of Sex Bias in India', *Population Studies*, 51(2), pp. 307–15.

Devi, Lakshmi, 2002, 'Education, Employment and Job Preference of Women in Kerala: A Micro Level Study', Discussion paper 42, Trivandrum: Kerala Research Programme on Local Level Development.

Dixon-Mueller, Ruth, 1993, *Population Policy and Women's Rights: Transforming Reproductive Choice*, Westport, CT: Praeger.

Dreze, J. and Sen, A. K., 1995, *India: Economic Development and Social Opportunity*, Delhi: OUP.

Dwyer, Daisy and Bruce, Judith, 1988, *A Home Divided: Women and Income in the Third World*, Palo Alto: Stanford University Press.

Dyson, T. and Moore, M., 1983, 'On Kinship Structure, Female Autonomy and Demographic Behavior in India', *Population and Development Review*, Vol. 9, No. 1, pp. 35–75.

Eapen, Mridul, 1992, 'Fertility and Female Labour Force Participation in Kerala', *Economic and Political Weekly*, Vol. 27, No. 40, pp. 2179.

____, 2004, 'Women and Work Mobility: Some Disquieting Evidences from the Indian Data', *Labour and Development*, Vol. 10, No. 2, pp. 167–87.

____ and Kodoth, Praveena, 2004, 'Family Structure, Women's Education and Work: Re-Examining The High Status of Women In Kerala', Swapna Mukhopadhyay and Ratna Sudarshan (eds.), *Tracking Gender Equity under Economic Reforms: Continuity and Change in South Asia*, New Delhi: Kali for Women & IDRC.

Gough, Kathleen, 1961, 'Nayars: Central Kerala; North Kerala; Tiyas: North Kerala; Mappillas: North Kerala', David M. Schneider and Kathleen Gough (eds.), *Matrilineal Kinship*, California: University of California Press.

Government of India, 2002, 'Selected Educational Statistics 2002–03', Department of Secondary and Higher Education, New Delhi: Ministry of Human Resource Development.

____, 2002a, *National Human Development Report-2001*, Planning Commission, New Delhi: Oxford University Press.

Government of Kerala, 2003, *Economic Review 2003*, Trivandrum: State Planning Board.

____, 2004, *Economic Review 2004*, February, Trivandrum: State Planning Board.

____, 2004a, *Women in Kerala-2004*, CD-Rom, Trivandrum: Directorate of Economics and Statistics.

Gulati, Leela, 1993, 'Population Ageing and Women in Kerala State, India', *Asia Pacific Population Journal*, Vol. 8, No. 1, pp. 53–63.

____ and Rajan, S. I., 1997, 'Women and Work in Kerala: A Comparison of 1981 and 1991 Censuses', *Indian Journal of Gender Studies*, 4(2), pp. 231–52.

Guilmoto, Z. Christopher and Rajan, S. I., 2002, 'District Level Estimates of Fertility from India's 2001 Census', *Economic and Political Weekly*, Vol. 37, No. 7, pp. 665–72.

International Clinical Epidemiologists Network, 2000, *India Safe: Studies of Abuse in the Family Environment in India-A Summary Report*, New Delhi.

International Institute for Population Sciences, 2000, *National Family Health Survey India, 1998–9*, Mumbai.

Jayasree, A.K., 1997, 'Gender Issues in Suicides: A Study among Suicide Attempters in Kerala State' (Manuscript), Trivandrum: Kerala Research Programme on Local Level Development.

Jeffrey, Robin, 1992, *Politics, Women and Well-being: How Kerala Became a Model*, London: Macmillan.

Kodoth, Praveena and Eapen, Mridul, 2005, 'Looking Beyond Gender Parity: Gender Inequalities of Some Dimensions of Well being in Kerala', *Economic and Political Weekly*, Vol. 40, No. 30, pp. 3278–86.

Krishnan, T.N., 1976, 'Demographic Transition in Kerala, Facts and Factors', *Economic and Political Weekly*, Vol. 11, Nos. 31, 32 and 33, pp. 1203–24.

Kumar, Rachel, 1992, 'Women, Work and Development: Issues in Female Labour Force Participation in Kerala', M. Phil Dissertation, Trivandrum: Centre for Development Studies.

____, 1994, 'Development and Women's Work in Kerala: Interaction and Paradoxes', *Economic and Political Weekly*, Vol. 29, Nos. 51 and 52, pp. 3249–54.

Mahmud, Simeen and Johnston, Anne M., 1994, 'Women's Status, Empowerment and Reproductive Outcomes', Gita Sen, Adrienne Germain, and Lincoln C. Chen (eds.), *Population Policies Reconsidered: Health, Empowerment and Rights*, Harvard Series on Population and International Health, Boston: Harvard School of Public Health.

Mason, K.O., 1984, *The Status of Women: A Review of Its Relationship to Fertility and Mortality*, New York: The Rockefeller Foundation.

Mathew, E.T., 1995, 'Educated Unemployment in Kerala: Some Socio-Economic Aspects', *Economic and Political Weekly*, Vol. 30, No. 6, pp. 325–35.

Miller, Barbara D., 1981, *The Endangered Sex: Neglect of Female Children in Rural North India*, Ithaca: Cornell University Press.

Mohamed, S., Rajan, S.I., Kumar, K. Anil and Mohammed, P.M. Saidu, 2002, 'Gender and Mental Health in Kerala', report submitted to New Delhi: Institute of Social Sciences under MIMAP-Gender Network Project (Phase II).

Moli, G.K., 2004, 'Labour Force in India: The Gender Gap', *Samyukta, Women's Initiatives*, Vol. 4, No. 2, July, pp. 53–67.

Nair, P. R. G., 1989, 'Universalization of Primary Education in Kerala', P. R. Panchamukhi (ed.), *Studies in Educational Reform in India, Vol.II, Part-I, Educational Reforms at Different Levels*, Bombay: Himalaya Publishing House.

_____, 1999, *Quality of School Education in Kerala: Dimensions and Determinants*, Kerala Research Programme on Local Level Development, Trivandrum: Centre for Development Studies.

Nandal, D.S., Khatri, R.S. and Kadian, R.S., 1987, 'Ageing Problems in the Structural Context', M. L. Sharma and T. M. Dak (eds.), *Ageing in India*, New Delhi: Ajanta Publications, pp. 106–16.

National Council of Educational Research and Training, 1998, *Sixth All India Educational Survey*, New Delhi.

National Sample Survey Organization, 1990, *Sarvekshana 1987–88*, September.

_____, 1996, *Sarvekshana 1993–94*, July–September.

_____, 2001, *Employment and Unemployment Situation in India 1999–2000, Report No. 458*, NSS 55th Round, July 1999–June 2000, Calcutta.

Prakash, B.A. and Abraham, M.P., 2004, 'Employment and Unemployment in Kerala', B.A. Prakash (ed.), *Kerala's Economic Development: Performance and Problems in the Post Liberalisation Period* 2nd edition, New Delhi: Sage Publications, pp. 82–123.

Prasad, Syam, 2005, 'A "Crisis in Making": The Pension System in India with Special Reference to Kerala', unpublished M.Phil. Dissertation, Trivandrum: Centre for Development Studies.

Rajan, S.I., Bhat, P.N. and Dyson, Tim, 1997, *Fertility and Mortality Transition in Kerala: A Historical Investigation*, New Delhi: Hindustan Publishing Corporation.

_____ and Zachariah, K.C., 1998, 'Long Term Implications of Low Fertility in Kerala', India', *Asia Pacific Population Journal*, 13 (3), pp. 41–56.

_____, Mishra, U.S. and Sarma, P.S., 1999, *India's Elderly: Burden or Challenge?*, New Delhi: Sage Publications.

_____, Sudha, S. and Nair, Mohanachandran, 2000, 'Fertility Decline and Worsening Gender Bias in India: Is Kerala no Longer an Exception?', *Development and Change*, Vol. 31, No. 4, pp. 1058–92.

——, 2002, 'Home Away from Home: A Survey of Oldage Homes and Inmates from Kerala, India', *Journal of Housing for the Elderly*, Vol. 16, Nos. 1 and 2, pp. 125–50.

—— and Kumar, Sanjay, 2003, 'Living Arrangements Among the Indian Elderly: New Evidence From the National Family Health Survey', *Economic and Political Weekly*, Vol. 38, No. 1, pp. 75–80.

——, Sarma, P.S. and Mishra, U.S., 2003a, 'Demography of Indian Ageing-2001–2051', Phoebe S. Liebig and S. Irudaya Rajan (eds.), *An Ageing India: Perspectives, Prospects, and Policies*, New York: The Haworth Press.

Rajan, S.I., 2006, 'Chronic Poverty Among Indian Elderly', Asha Kapur Mehta and Andrew Sheperd (eds.), *Chronic Poverty and Development Policy in India*, New Delhi: Sage Publications, pp. 168–96.

—— and Aliyar, Sabu, 2004, 'Gender Ageing and Social Security', *Samyukta, Women's Initiatives*, Vol. 4, No. 2, July, Trivandrum, pp. 68–87.

Ramachandran, V.K., 1996, 'On Kerala's Development Achievements', J. Dreze and A.K. Sen, (eds.), *Indian Development: Selected Regional Perspectives*, New Delhi: Oxford University Press, pp. 268–322.

Ratcliffe, J., 1978, 'Social Justice and Demographic Transition: Lessons from India's Kerala State', *International Journal of Health Services*, Vol. 8, No. 1, pp. 123–44.

Raza, Mooniz and Agarwal, Y., 1984, 'Higher Education in India—The Regional Dimension', New Delhi: National Institute of Educational Planning and Administration, Occasional Paper 9.

Registrar General, 2001, 'Provisional Population Totals, Census of India Series 1, India', Paper 1 of 2001, New Delhi.

Registrar General and Census Commissioner, 2004, *Report and Tables on Age, Census of India 2001, Series-1*, New Delhi.

Registrar General, 2005, *SRS Bulletin-Sample Registration System* Vol. 39, No. 1, April, New Delhi: Vital Statistics Division.

Saradamoni, K., 1994, 'Women, Kerala and some Development issues', *Economic and Political Weekly*, Vol. 29, No. 9, pp. 501–9.

——, 1999, *Matriliny Transformed: Family, Law and Ideology in Twentieth Century Travancore*, New Delhi: Sage Publications.

Sebastian, Alice, 2005, 'Educated Unemployment and Women in Kerala', Unpublished M.Phil. Dissertation, Trivandrum: Centre for Development Studies.

Sen, A. K., 1990, 'Gender and Cooperative Conflicts', Irene Tinker (ed.), *Persistent Inequalities: Women and World Development*, New York: Oxford University Press.

Sreerupa, 2006, 'Gender, Ageing and Widowhood: Health Vulnerability and Socio-economic Influences', Unpublished M.Phil. Dissertation, Trivandrum: Centre for Development Studies.

Sudha, S., Khanna, S., Rajan, S.I. and Srivastava, Roma, forthcoming, 'Traditions in Transformation: Gender Bias among the Nairs of Kerala', *Journal of Family History.*

Tilak, J.B.J. and Bhatt, 1989, 'Educational Development in Haryana: An Inter District Analysis', *Margin,* Vol. 22, Nos.1&2, pp. 108–23.

United Nations, 1991, 'Advancement of Women: Convention On The Elimination of All Forms of Discrimination Against Women', *Report of the Secretary-General,* General Assembly, New York: United Nations.

Unni, Jeemol, 1996, 'Who is Schooled and Why? Gender Differentials in Education', Ahmedabad: Gujarat Institute of Development and Research, Working Paper 73.

Visaria, Leela, 2002, 'Deficit of Women in India: Magnitude, Trends, Regional Variations and Determinants', *The National Medical Journal of India,* 15, Supplement 1, pp. 19–25.

Wadhwa, Soma, 2004, 'The Hoax of God's Own Country', *Outlook,* 12 July.

Youssef, Nadia H., 1982, 'The Interrelationship Between the Division of Labour in the Household, Women's Roles and their Impact on Fertility', R. Anker, M. Buvinic and N.H. Youssef (eds.), *Women's Roles and Population Trends in the Third World,* London: Croom Helm.

Zachariah, K.C., Rajan, S.I., Sharma, P.S., Navaneetham, K., Nair, S. and Mishra, U.S., 1994, *Demographic Transition in Kerala on the 1980's,* Trivandrum: Centre for Development Studies.

____ and Rajan, S. I., 1997, *Kerala's Demographic Transition: Determinants and Consequences,* New Delhi: Sage Publications.

Zachariah, K.C., 1998, 'Models of Development and Demographic Change—A Case Study of Kerala', *Demography India,* Vol. 27, No. 1, pp. 71–89.

____, Mathew, E.T. and Rajan, S.I., 2003, *Dynamics of Migration in Kerala: Dimensions, Differentials and consequences,* New Delhi: Orient Longman.

____ and Rajan, S.I., 2004, 'Gulf Revisited Economic Consequences of Emigration From Kerala, Emigration and Unemployment', Working Paper 363, Trivandrum: Centre for Development Studies.

____, 2005, 'Unemployment in Kerala at the Turn of the Century: Insights from CDS Gulf Migration Studies', Working Paper 374, Trivandrum: Centre for Development Studies.

chapter three

Mental Health, Gender Ideology and Women's Status in Kerala

Swapna Mukhopadhyay, Jayanti Basu and S. Irudaya Rajan

I INTRODUCTION

Studies on mental health have generally been the prerogative of mental health experts, outside the ambit of general social science research. However, the search for a class of relatively context-free set of gender development indicators prompted the inclusion of the mental health aspect of human well-being as an integral part of Gender Network research agenda.[1] An inquiry into the mental health scenario in Kerala was deemed important in view of the high levels of conventional gender development indicators such as high female literacy levels and low levels of maternal mortality, in contrast to disturbing evidence of declining infant sex ratios, rising incidence of dowry and domestic violence. This paper analyses some of the findings of a survey of mental health carried out on a representative sample of over five thousand men and women from one thousand households spread across fourteen districts of Kerala. The focus of the survey is to understand how the gender differentiated status of mental health relates to differences in household and

[1]This was initially prompted by the understanding that, cutting across social contexts, violence against women, and the credible threat of such violence can result in gender-based stress and anxiety. Since violence appears to be the most widespread manifestation of unequal power relations between men and women, gender-differentiated mental health indicators can be useful in analysing issues of women's status. See Mukhopadhyay (2003) and chapter 1 in this volume for a more detailed exposition of these ideas.

individual characteristics. It also looks at the kind of links it has with the internalized notions of gender ideology in Kerala society.

While mental health, just as physical health, should be deemed to be an integral dimension of the well-being of an individual, independent of gender, on the face of it, there is no a priori reason to expect that the status of women in a particular community will have a one-to-one correspondence with gender-differentiated status of mental health within it, unless contextual specificities suggest otherwise. To cite an example, let us take that one indicator of women's status that seems to cut across differences in class and caste divides: i.e., violence against women. Assuming that violence against women in its broader sense is a major indicator of the low status of women in a society, the existence and severity of actual perpetrated violence, and credible threat of such violence along with the associated stress and anxiety that it entails, will undoubtedly increase levels of mental distress among women in that society. In such situations, distress can be taken as a sure indicator of the low status of women. However, the extent of recorded levels of distress measured by standard indicators of mental health may depend on many other factors and may well vary from one situation to another even after correcting for environmental differences, such as differences in material levels of living. If such violence is perceived to be unjust or excessive by the women, levels of distress are likely to be higher, ceteris paribus, than otherwise. In situations where both men and women subscribe to the notion of a certain hierarchy in gender relations, and perceive relatively mild forms of violence to be the norm rather than the exception, recorded levels of mental distress and psychological well being on account of this factor may not be affected too much. Hence the importance of understanding gender role ideology as a determinant of the levels of stress and, consequently, of the recorded levels of mental health indicators.

The study needs to be placed in the perspective of the present scenario of the mental health status of women and men. Gender balance in the prevalence of mental disorders is notoriously asymmetric all over the world (Busfield 1996; Malik 1993; WHO 2000). Women predominate in stress related symptoms, especially, depressive and anxiety disorders, and body image related problems like eating disorders (Russo 1990; McIntyre and Hunt 1997). Recent literature points to the fact that the negative mental health status of women is not so much due to biological reasons as due to personal, social and political factors (Lorber 1997). In this regard, the role of everyday difficulties and negative life events (Bolger et al. 1989; Weissman et al. 1993), violence and abuse (Ratner 1993; Sugarman and Frankel 1996), sexist discrimination (Landrine et al. 1995), and finally, role conflict and multiple roles (Cleary and Mechanic 1983; Gove 1979; Pearlin 1975) have been emphasized. There is, however, an increasing body of literature that shows that multiple roles among women may contribute to positive mental health as well (Adelman 1994; Helson et al. 1990).

Indeed, the emerging literature on mental health increasingly reveals the need to study separately, the negative aspects of mental health or distress and its positive aspects, i.e., wellness, for a comprehensive understanding of mental health status. Absence of disease is not synonymous with wellness. While disease is the presence of distressing symptoms, wellness is the presence of happiness and the ability to experience a good quality of life. In fact, the two variables are only moderately negatively correlated and wellness is recognized as a significant factor in the overall mental health status (Diener et al. 1997). The available studies also tend to yield contradictory results, in so far as the same person may come up with higher levels of stress as well as wellness indicators. However, gender difference has been scrutinized with care in cases of distress and disease, and rarely in cases of wellness.

This paper analyses the data generated by the Kerala Mental Health Survey to understand the variations in the mental health status of men and women in Kerala in terms of a range of socio-economic indicators. Simultaneously, the paper investigates the linkages between a couple of standard mental health indicators and the ideology of gender relations subscribed to by men and women in the sample. An index of gender ideology has been especially constructed for this study.

II THE KERALA MENTAL HEALTH SURVEY (KMHS)

Background

The Kerala Mental Health Survey (KMHS) was conducted in 2002, on a sample of 1000 households spread over all fourteen districts of Kerala.[2] This was a representatively selected 10 per cent sub-sample of a sample of 10,000 households selected for the Kerala Migration

[2]The Kerala Mental Health Study (KMHS) survey instrument was prepared by the Gender Network research team and the survey was carried out across the state by a team of researchers under the supervision of Dr E. Mohamed, Director of Ansari Hospital, Trissur district, Kerala. We are grateful to Dr

Survey conducted by the Centre for Development Studies in 1998. The survey questionnaire in KMHS was given to all members in the selected households in the 12–60 years age groups, as well as to those members of the 60-plus age groups who were willing to answer the questions. The survey collected information on three sets of variables:

(i) Socio-economic variables

(ii) Levels of psychological distress as well as of mental well-being of the individuals for construction of two mental health indicators, GHQ and SUBI respectively.

(iii) Perceptions and attitudes of the individuals on gender relations and gender ideology.

The questions on the socio-economic variables elicited information on variables such as age, education, marital status, occupation and labour status categories of individuals, as well as economic conditions and demographic profiles of households to which they belonged.

On mental health, information was collected for the construction of two standard instruments widely used in Applied Psychological research. The first is General Health Questionnaire (GHQ). Originally a 60-question instrument (Goldberg and Hiller 1979), the version used here is the 12-question 'best items' set, which has found wide application in India and abroad in studies of psychological distress. The GHQ score has been used both as a dimensional measure of psychological stress as well as an indicator of potential clinical psychiatric cases in case it exceeds a specified threshold level. In the 12-item version of GHQ, this threshold level has been identified as 2; anybody having a score higher than 2 is a potential clinical psychiatric case.

The second mental health indicator on which data have been collected is the Subjective Well Being Inventory (SUBI), which is designed to capture the mental well being of the interviewee. The short version of the original 40-item questionnaire (Sell and Nagpal 1992) used in this study is the 9-item version, which can be broken into three factors: general well-being, expectation achievement congruence, and confidence in coping. As with GHQ, a higher SUBI score indicates a lower level of mental well-being.

It may be mentioned here that the SUBI and GHQ scores of a

Mohamed and his team of dedicated researchers for conducting the survey and to Professor K.C.Zachariah of the Centre for Development Studies for expert advice on sample selection. The tables reported in this section of the paper are taken from the Report of the KMHS, submitted to ISST in December 2002. For more details, please see Mohamed et al., 2002.

population need not generate the same rankings. In other words, a person may be subjected to a relatively higher degree of mental stress manifested in a high GHQ score, as compared to another, but may have a better sense of well-being than the latter, in terms of SUBI. This may well be the result of a better coping ability of the former to handle stress and anxiety, as compared to the latter. General Health Questionnaire and SUBI are two indices that explore two interlinked but essentially separate dimensions of mental health. They are neither collinear with, nor are they orthogonal to each other. In this study we present results based on both the indices.

The KMHS also collected information on a third set of variables. This consists of perceptions, attitudes and the ideology of the interviewees on gender relations in society. This set of 15 questions on gender ideology, was pilot tested in the district of Thrissur and then administered to the whole sample. A sub-sample of 200 households was randomly selected from the original 1000 for standardizing the questionnaire. The standardized instrument comprising 8 questions was administered to the remaining 800 households to obtain the Gender Ideology scores.[3] The analysis involving GI scores reported in Section 3 of this paper pertains to the sample of these 800 households and not the original 1000.

Levels of Perceived Well-Being (SUBI)

As mentioned earlier, the Kerala Mental Health Survey (KMHS) data set consists of a sample of 1000 households (Table 3.1)—consisting of 5450 persons, 2740 males and 2710 females—randomly selected from a 10,000-household representative sample used in an earlier survey, the Kerala Migration Survey (KMS). This was carried out in the state by the Centre for Development Studies in Thiruvananthipuram, in 1998 (for more details, see Zachariah, Mathew and Rajan 2003).

The results reported in this section reflect the findings of the Kerala Mental Health Survey (2002). Tabular analysis of the data suggests the following broad patterns.

Broad patterns emerging from tabulations of levels of perceived well-being (SUBI)

In terms of perceived psychological well-being, the study suggests that men are clearly better off than their female counterparts, with recorded SUBI scores for men being consistently lower than those

[3]Cf. Appendix

Table 3.1 Sample Size by District: KMS and KMHS[4]

District	*No of Households*	*KMS (1998)*	*KMHS (2002)*
Kasaragod	181,667	330	30
Kannur	371,221	673	72
Wayanad	134,654	244	30
Kozhikode	456,673	828	79
Malappuram	477,292	866	90
Palakkad	444,998	897	80
Thrissur	522,159	947	99
Ernakulam	555,657	1,008	96
Idukki	232,995	423	40
Kottayam	361,813	656	64
Alappuzha	405,210	735	70
Pathanamthitta	259,629	471	50
Kollam	489,774	888	90
Thriuvananthapuram	619,558	1,124	110
KERALA	**5,513,300**	**10,090**	**1000**

KMS: Kerala Migration Survey, 1998
KMHS: Kerala Mental Health Survey, 2002

for women: the average difference in the male and female scores being statistically significant at 1 per cent level.[5]

In general, there is an inverse trend in SUBI scores when mapped against increasing age. This suggests that the level of psychological well-being declines as people grow older, for both males and females for most parts of the distribution. However there is a difference. For men, the trend is almost monotonic until the mid-fifties after which, the level of well-being, in fact, shows a marginal improvement. For women, the ride through the life cycle is anything but smooth. First, there is a marked dip in the level of perceived well-being for women in the 25–34 year age group, coinciding with the major chunk of child bearing, and rearing years, and second, for women in the oldest categories, there is, again, a sharp dip in the recorded levels of well-being (Table 3.2). This is reinforced by the fact that the trend rate of age-induced decline in well-being is significantly higher for women than for men. Older women have amongst the lowest levels of well-being in the sample.

[4]Report of KMHS submitted to ISST.
[5]Report of KMHS submitted to ISST.

If one tabulates men and women by their marital status, the 'happiest' in both sexes are those that are unmarried, happier than those that are married. However, the worst off by far, are the widows. The interesting thing to note here is that, although the result is not statistically significant, the only marital status category in which women are relatively happier than men, is the one in which they are divorced. Divorced women record a better level of well-being than their male counterparts (Table 3.3).

With regard to work status, farmers and labourers are the worst off in terms of perceived well-being, and government servants are the happiest of the lot; a clear reflection of the relative economic well-being of the households, both in terms of income levels and income security (Table 3.4).

Table 3.2 Index of Subjective Well-being by Age and Sex in Kerala, 2002[6]

Age	*Male*	*Female*	Mean of the Scores		*t value*
			Male	*Female*	
15–24	344	343	16.41	16.88	-1.639
25–34	269	313	17.21	19.75	-1.507
35–44	237	313	17.63	18.13	-2.285
45–54	233	277	18.19	18.54	-0.885
55+	225	231	17.80	19.64	-4.955*

* Significant at 1 % level.

Table 3.3 Index of Subjective Well-being by Sex and Marital Status in Kerala, 2002[7]

Marital Status	*Male*	*Female*	Mean of the Scores		*t value*
			Male	*Female*	
Unmarried	99	79	15.52	16.82	-2.272**
Married	1086	1117	17.33	17.89	-3.286*
Widowed	98	220	18.75	19.81	-1.715***
Divorced	10	24	19.40	17.90	1.123

* Significant at 1% level; ** Significant at 5 % level; *** Significant at 10% level

[6]Report of KMHS submitted to ISST.
[7]Report of KMHS submitted to ISST.

Table 3.4 Index of Subjective Well-being by Work Status and Sex in Kerala, 2002[8]

Work Status	*Male*	*Female*	Mean of the Scores		*t value*
			Male	*Female*	
Government	80	30	14.57	16.80	-2.082***
Private	86	32	16.59	17.84	-1.323
Self-employed	261	42	17.67	19.40	-2.289***
Farmers	121	53	18.51	20.51	-2.792**
Labourers	374	77	17.10	20.55	-5.324*
Unemployed	186	81	17.80	17.84	-0.220
Student	171	146	15.61	16.16	-1.494
House work	18	1012	17.83	18.17	-0.198

* Highly Significant; ** Significant at 1 % level; *** Significant at 5% level

In the specific context of this paper when one maps gender disparities with regard to perceived psychological well-being against the background of household poverty and household income insecurity, poor women display the highest SUBI levels, or in other words, they are the worst off in terms of perceived well-being. Gender disparities also go up sharply as one moves down the job ladder. This is also evident when one tabulates male and female levels of well-being against other categories that are highly correlated with incomes. Scheduled Castes, Scheduled Tribes and Ezavahs, for instance, have among the highest SUBI levels. Gender disparities also rise steadily as one moves down the caste scale, suggesting very low levels of well-being, especially for the women from these caste groups (Table 3.5).[9]

It would be legitimate to generalize from these findings, that while poverty adversely affects the psychological well-being of all members of a household, the relative severity of the impact of poverty on women increases steadily, vis-à-vis men, as households get poorer.

In terms of regions in the state, there is a clear indication that the worst average levels of well-being for both men and women are in the southern districts of Kerala. The average levels of well-being get increasingly better as one moves to the central and then, to the northern districts. It would be interesting to map this finding against the distribution of caste, religious and ethnic groups across the various regions of the state.

[8]Report of KMHS submitted to ISST.

[9]Report of KMHS submitted to ISST.

Table 3.5 Index of Subjective Well-being by Religion and Caste in Kerala, 2002

Religion/Caste	*Male*	*Female*	Mean of the Scores		*t value*
			Male	*Female*	
SC/ST	94	109	18.27	18.76	-0.931
Nair	133	143	16.68	17.86	-2.43**
Ezhava	292	322	17.95	18.07	-0.354
Syrian X'ans	138	135	16.57	17.71	-2.531**
Other X'ans	151	180	17.20	18.48	-2.835*
Muslims	258	335	17.35	17.62	-0.720
Others	173	173	17.35	17.84	-1.200

* Significant at 1% level; ** Significant at 5 % level

An insightful result thrown up by the survey is that, while poverty is a primary cause of subjective ill-being for both men and women, it is not the only cause. The importance of non-economic factors in defining women's well-being is brought out sharply when one tabulates gender disparities in mental health indicators by community membership. Although gender disparities in perceived well-being are a rising function of the poverty of households, the largest disparities in SUBI levels turn out not to be within the poorest households, but among communities such as Syrian Christians and Nairs, communities which have traditionally belonged to the affluent class.[10]

Broad patterns emerging from tabulations of levels of mental distress (GHQ)

There are several areas where tabulations of GHQ scores show the same patterns as those of SUBI scores. With SUBI, women on an average showed higher scores, and therefore, lower levels of subjective well-being. In GHQ as well, women on an average fared worse than men

Table 3.6 Index of Mental Health in Kerala by Sex, 2002

Gender	*Total*	*Score Mean*	*t value*
Male	1308	1.81	-4.518*
Female	1477	2.33	

* Highly Significant.

[10]Report of KMHS submitted to ISST.

(Table 3.6). Women showed higher levels of recorded GHQ than men, suggesting that women experience higher degrees of mental stress and anxiety.

General Health Questionnaire mapped against some of the socio-economic variables reveal some broad patterns.

Growing old is synonymous with greater mental stress. As with SUBI, here too, the descent with age into a state of greater anxiety and stress is steeper for women, with old women displaying the worst levels of GHQ.

As with SUBI, the marital status of a person is linked with GHQ. Marriage, on an average, raises GHQ levels. The worst off, once again, are widowed women, who incidentally, are also likely to be the oldest. At the same time, if a woman is divorced, or separated, the level of stress rises significantly for her too; similar trends are not noticeable in the sample for men (Table 3.7).

Higher levels of education generally reduce stress for both men and women. Once again, this may partly be a reflection of the relative economic prosperity of the educated. What is interesting to note here is that, while the general trend is observable for both men and women, for the latter, there is unevenness in the two-way relationship between education and mental distress. This is manifested in a sharp peak in mental distress for women who have primary education, making them almost as stressed out, on an average, as illiterate women (Table 3.8).

This phenomenon needs to be investigated further, but it seems to suggest that literacy, by itself, does not result in a reduction of the levels of stress of Kerala women in the same manner, or to the same degree, as it does for men. This could very well be a reflection

Table 3.7 Index of Mental Health in Kerala by Marital Status, 2002[11]

Marital Status	*Male*	*Female*	Mean of the Scores		*t value*
			Male	*Female*	
Unmarried	99	79	1.22	1.35	-0.354
Married	1086	1117	1.78	2.28	-3.966*
Widowed	98	220	2.50	3.62	-2.332**
Divorced	10	24	1.90	2.70	-0.897

* Highly Significant; ** Significant at 5 % level

[11]Report of KMHS submitted to ISST.

of the fact that what literacy can do as an instrument of control over the life situation of an individual may be very different for women from what it is for men.

Another difference in the impact of education and labour market variables on levels of stress and anxiety for men and women, is thrown up by the data on unemployment. Unemployed women are far more stressed out than unemployed men, and a large percentage of the former happen to be educated (Table 3.9).

Table 3.8 Index of Mental Health in Kerala by Educational Attainment, 2002[12]

Educational Attainment	*Male*	*Female*	Mean of the Scores *Male*	Mean of the Scores *Female*	*t value*
Illiterate	42	123	3.88	3.30	0.652
Literate	34	33	3.45	3.21	0.291
Primary	188	246	2.30	3.48	-2.023**
Middle	598	658	1.83	2.32	-2.851*
Secondary	330	321	1.14	1.56	-2.253**
Degree	116	94	0.84	1.38	-1.613

* Significant at 1% level; ** Significant at 5 % level

Table 3.9 Index of Mental Health in Kerala by Work Status, 2002[13]

Employment Status	*Male*	*Female*	Mean of the Scores *Male*	Mean of the Scores *Female*	*t value*
Government	80	30	0.700	2.30	-2.227***
Private	86	32	1.06	2.78	-2.768**
Self-employed	261	42	1.02	3.33	-4.175*
Farmers	121	53	2.13	3.51	-1.917****
Labourers	374	77	1.05	3.96	-5.629*
Unemployed	186	81	1.82	3.13	-2.60**
Student	171	146	0.88	0.91	-0.135
House work	18	1012	4.50	2.5	1.635

* Highly Significant; ** Significant at 1 % level; *** Significant at 5% level: **** Significant at 10% level

[12]Report of KMHS submitted to ISST.
[13]Report of KMHS submitted to ISST.

GENDER IDEOLOGY AND MENTAL HEALTH

A striking feature of the sample is the very high percentages (women more than men) that show up with potentially problematic mental health characteristics in the sample population. The percentage of men scoring above the cut-off point in GHQ is 43.72% while that of women is 49.80%. The situation with the wellness index is worse, with 50.72% of men and an alarming 56.65% of women scoring above the cut-off point in the SUBI scale. Compared with national and international figures, the incidence of mental stress and mental illness appear to be significantly worse for the population of Kerala. This, by itself, is a cause for concern. Women, of course, are worse than men in terms of both indices, which is, more or less, a common scenario.

Direct questioning suggests that the household economic situation is a prime cause for stress and anxiety, in both men and women. This could very well be so, especially where relatively high levels of education push up expectations for high incomes. These expectations cannot be realized due to low levels of general economic development: a scenario that could be said to characterize the Kerala situation. Could gender role ideology also have a similar role to play? A number of earlier studies abroad have indicated that conservative upbringing and socialization can lead to internalization of stereotyped gender role ideologies. This, in turn, can lead to negative self-evaluation among women causing negative stress tolerance and enhanced vulnerability to distress and disorders (Belk and Snell 1989; Ruble et al. 1993; Kuiper and Dance 1994). It has also been observed that gender role ideologies operate more intensely to influence mental health status in women than in men (Cameron and Lalonde 2001).

Most of these studies have been carried out in the context of western societies. Systematic analysis of interlinkages between the status of mental health of a population and the gender ideology it subscribes to—especially gender differences in such linkages—are rare in the context of Indian society. One exception to this is the study by Davar (1999), which highlighted the way Indian women are differentiated from men in prevalence, aetiology, and the availability of mental health services. Davar also demonstrates the inconsistency and lack of normativity of the available psychiatric researches in this context, making comparison across provinces difficult. In Kolkata, two studies have been conducted to relate gender role with mental health among 'normal' young adults (Basu 2004), and with psychiatric patients (Basu 2003). These two studies demonstrate how inconsistent gender role messages are integrated into the identity of women, and in turn, associated with their mental health status. However, considering the complicated emotional and social issues involved in the matter, the studies mentioned above are, at best, indicative and serve merely to posit relevant questions for further research.

As seen in Table 3.10 below, GI scores for men and women in the Kerala Mental Health Survey come up with the evidence of women subscribing to a more patriarchal gender ideology than men on an average, with the difference being statistically quite significant.

Table 3.10 Index of Gender Ideology in Kerala by Sex, 2002[14]

Gender	*Total*	*Score Mean*	*t value*
Male	1308	6.68	-3.509*
Female	1477	7.11	

* Highly Significant.

Does this have anything to do with the enigma surrounding the issue of women's status in Kerala?

Clearly the issues involved are complex. The KMHS data provides us with the basic ingredients to carry out a preliminary analysis of some of these questions. However, the two-dimensional tables presented in the earlier section may very well conceal the complexities of the multiple dimensionalities of the data. The following section presents the results of some multivariate statistical analysis carried out with the data to see the relationship between gender ideology and the gender-differentiated status of mental health indicators.

III A STATISTICAL FORMAT FOR ANALYSIS

A number of regressions were run to unearth the statistical relationships between various socio-economic variables, gender ideology and the status of mental health for the total sample, and for men and women separately. The sample consists of 1241 persons, 988 males and 1241 females, from 800 households out of the original 1000 after deleting the 200 randomly chosen households which were used to construct the standardized Gender Ideology (GI) Index.[15] Apart from the socio-economic variables, standardized gender ideology scores have been used as an independent variable in explaining variations in the status

[14]Report of KMHS submitted to ISST.

[15]See Appendix 3.1 on the construction of the GI index.

of mental health. We have used the total GI scores over the eight questions selected during the standardization process in the reported equations, although separate equations were run using the two separate clusters of six and two questions respectively but have not been reported here. Four different specifications of the dependent variable have been used. These are:

GHQ scores ranging from 0 to 12,

GHQD: A dummy variable which takes the value 1 when GHQ score is less than or equal to 2, and is 0 otherwise,

SUBI scores ranging from 9 to 27,

SUBID: A dummy variable which takes the value 1 when SUBI score is less than or equal to 16, and is 0 otherwise.

The socio-economic variables which have been used in addition to the GI score as explanatory variables are:

Age and age-squared, educational status, marital status, labour force status, economic status of the household, region within the state, religion/caste and sex of the respondent, for equations using the combined sample of men and women respondents.[16]

With the status of mental health of the individual as the dependent variable, several equations were run using combinations of the above variables to explore the explanatory power of various model specifications. Since at least two of the specifications for the dependent variable, i.e., GHQD and SUBID, are binary variables, Probit and Logit models appropriate for such cases were used. The reported results for Probit equations are for marginal coefficients. A few results on Odds Ratios using the Logit specification have also been given for the purpose of comparison. Appendix 3.1 contains a sample of equations that were run to assess the linkages between the mental health indicators and the gender ideology index, given other socio-economic characteristics of the interviewees as outlined in the variable chart in the appendix.

As noted above, the nature of association between mental health indicators and other variables as outlined in the descriptions in the earlier section, is based on two-way tabulations of the data. While useful in themselves, these two-way classifications cannot take into account the effect of other variables in the system that may be simultaneously impacting both. This is the primary reason why one goes in for multivariate analysis in such situations, and if possible, to simultaneous systems as well. The analysis carried out here is, however, restricted to single equations regressions. There is, as yet,

[16]Cf. Appendix 3.1 for the variable chart and a sample of the equations.

no well-established 'theory' in the area connecting variables such as 'gender ideology' and 'status of mental health' for instance, to warrant the construction of elaborate simultaneous systems. As an expository analysis seeking to investigate statistical associations, if any, between some of these variables, this would have been too ambitious a project to start with. Even while opting for a single equation model, however, we do experiment with some alternative model and variable specifications within the single equation format, and come up with some striking results. These are reported in Appendix 3.2 of this paper. The nature of association that emerges between the dependent variable, i.e., various measures of mental stress as well as of perceived mental well-being with the major explanatory variables in these equations, turns out to be pretty robust. The following paragraphs summarize the broad nature of associations that emerge between the mental health indicators and various explanatory variables from the estimated equations These are based on the results of the regressions reported in the Appendix 3.2 of the paper. The reason behind reporting several estimated equations in the Appendix is to underline the robustness of some crucial associations between some of the key variables that emerge, independent of variable or model specifications.

Summary of Results

Gender Ideology

All the equations point to the striking result showing a significant relationship of the standardized gender ideology indicator with all the four specifications of mental health status as the dependent variable. This is true for the equations run separately for men and women, and also for those that use the whole sample with a sex dummy as an explanatory variable. This holds good for both the Probit and Logit models. The significance of the gender variable is highest among all the explanatory variables in all the specifications tried out with this data. The results strongly suggest that given other things, a higher gender ideology score (i.e., holding more orthodox views on gender roles and norms) leads to higher levels of GHQ (greater stress and anxiety) and higher SUBI (lower levels of perceived mental well-being). It also raises the probability of a person going beyond the 'threshold' levels in terms of both the mental health indicators, as a potential psychiatric case. The results suggest that one percentage point rise in the GI score could worsen the indicators of mental health anywhere by a factor of two to three percentage points.

Considering that the relationship in the equations between gender ideology and mental health is stronger for women than men in terms of significance levels, and also the fact that the marginal coefficients in Probit models and the odds ratios in the Logit models are fairly consistently higher for women than for men, one can say that subscribing to an orthodox gender ideology does more harm to women than to men. Given that the gender ideology scores in the sampled population are worse for women than for men, this could be one strong reason why Kerala women are worse off in terms of mental health than Kerala men in the sample.

Age

Broadly speaking, the results show that the status of mental health of individuals declines as they grow older, since all equations have a positive and significant coefficient for the age variable. The age-squared variable, however, is fairly consistent with negative, though largely insignificant, coefficients in the equations. Even if these were statistically significant, the associated values of the coefficients in the original equations in most cases are such that the negative effect of the latter is unlikely to show up within the average life span of the sampled population. This suggests that, for all practical purposes, the observed relationship between mental health status and age is negative, with mental health indicators becoming increasingly worse as one gets older.

The effect of other variables on the status of mental health of men and women can be read from the equations. While they broadly corroborate the results obtained from the tabular analysis of the data presented in Section II above, there are some interesting details that can be read from the multivariate analysis results. These details could not be found through two way tabular analyses where variations in other variables cannot be held constant.

Education

The impact of education on mental health is, by and large, positive, but there are subtle differences between men and women. While GHQ and SUBI decrease, i.e. status of mental health improves with higher levels of education, the impact is more pronounced for men than for women. In fact for women, the education variable is not significant before one crosses the level of secondary education. However, when we study the effect of education on the dichotomized GHQ and SUBI, it appears that with rising educational levels, the possibility of crossing the 'threshold' is averted with higher probability for women than for men. This tendency is stronger in case of the SUBI dummy than for the GHQ dummy.

One could perhaps, hypothesize from these results that being educated per se does not benefit women as much as men in terms of mental health parameters, until one crosses the secondary level. It may be noted that a similar finding had surfaced from preliminary tabular analysis of the thousand household data reported in Section II of the paper.

Marital Status

The marital status variable exhibits significance for men, although the situation is different for women. Compared to those in the unmarried category, GHQ and SUBI scores are significantly higher for divorced and widowed women. However, they are not significant for either the married women or men in any of the other categories.

The results are somewhat different when we look at the dichotomized GHQ and SUBI. These versions of the equations indicate that being divorced, widowed or separated, as opposed to being unmarried or currently married, could increase the propensity for crossing threshold levels, especially in terms of perceived mental well-being, in both men and women. This could mean that given other things, marriage may exacerbate potential psychiatric problems. But this hypothesis would clearly need more evidence to be substantiated.

Work Status

The impact of work status on mental health is not the same for men and women. With regular salaried workers as the base, this variable is insignificant for men for all the other categories. However, for women, being a student or being involved in domestic work, more so the former than the latter, raises the level of well-being as compared to holding a secure job (see Table 3.4). This is an interesting result and needs further probing, especially since it does not turn out to be robust with respect to model specification (Cf. Table 3.2). It may be noted that work status turns out to be a more significant variable for men than women in case of the dichotomized mental health indicators. Men in low status and insecure jobs are more prone to critical levels of mental stress and lower well-being than women. (see Tables 3.4 and 3.9).

Economic Status

The broad relationship between better mental health and higher economic status of the household is positive. As the economic status of the household goes down, levels of mental distress and ill-being go up. However this effect is most evident when one compares the richest households with the poorest, and is strengthened when one looks at the dichotomized mental health indicators. Men and women react differently to the economic status of the household, in terms of threshold levels of mental distress and ill being. Women appear to be more prone to distress (higher GHQ) while men seem to suffer from a greater sense of ill-being (higher SUBI).

Caste/Religion Groups

Taking the SC/ST category as the base group, regressions were run to study the differential effects of caste/religion categories on mental health indicators. The results suggest that there are no significant, and consistent marginal variations in the mental health status across these groups, although in terms of significance of the t-values, caste divisions seem to be more significant predictors of mental health status for men than for women (see Tables A3.1.1–A3.1.5).

Region

The state has been divided into three regions: south, central and north. This has been done to broadly reflect the differences in the ethnic and cultural characteristics of the population in these locations. The effect of regional variations is more prominent for women than for men. This also emerges in dimensional differences in the GHQ and SUBI scores rather than in the assessment of potential threshold or critical levels of mental ill-being and distress. For women, the results are quite clear. Controlling for other variables, the impact of being located in the southern region is the least beneficial for the mental health status of women. Things get better as one moves from the south to the central region, and to the north. One would perhaps need to look beyond the crude regional breakdown, into the differential distributional profiles of communities and ethnic groups in these regions, to understand the implications of this result.

Sex Dummy

Some of the equations were run for the whole sample with an intercept dummy to represent the sex of the individual. An example of this set of results is reproduced in Appendix Table A3.2.5. Without any exception, the sex dummy shows a positive and significant coefficient in all the equations, suggesting that both mental distress and mental ill-being indicators are higher for women.

IV CONCLUDING OBSERVATIONS

The results of the multivariate regressions suggest a strong statistical association between orthodox gender ideology and the status of mental health and perceived well-being of the individual, keeping other factors constant. Women also exhibit a higher degree of anxiety and mental stress, and lower levels of psychological well-being than men, but that is a common finding the world over, and not specific to the Kerala situation. There are two striking features about these results though. One, as noted above, women in our sample are significantly more orthodox than men in terms of their gender ideology; and two, as the results of the multivariate regressions clearly suggest, high level of gender orthodoxy is a strong determinant of low levels of mental well-being. This is true for both men and women, but more so for women than for men. This suggests that perhaps some portion of the gender differentials in levels of mental well-being in Kerala can be traced to higher levels of gender orthodoxy of Kerala women.

This is a rather significant finding. Tabular analysis of the data in section II above has suggested a number of factors that may have contributed to the stress levels of women. The stress brought about by reproductive responsibilities is manifested in higher GHQ levels among married women in the reproductive age group. Old age and poverty manifest themselves in high levels of gendered patterns of psychological ill being. Even literacy may heighten women's stress levels relative to that of men. This is due to the fact that literacy may raise expectations without adequate outlets for self-expression and opportunities for exercising control over one's life. The one factor already mentioned above that has repeatedly come out with the highest significance levels as a determinant of mental ill being in both men and women—more so for women than men—is the high level of gender orthodoxy.

This also, to a certain extent answers the contradiction involved in the issue of women's status in Kerala. High levels of conventional gender development indicators have not translated into a more liberated gender ideology for the Kerala women, or men, for that matter. The straitjacket of a stereotypical gender ideology has kept the women in a time warp as it were and may very well have done so at the cost of heightened levels of mental distress and ill being. These are complex issues and need more coordinated research. The study has hopefully been able to highlight the relevance of some commonly neglected facets of women's status in the state, which need to be explored at greater depth.

APPENDIX 3.1

Construction of the Gender Role Ideology Scale

A scale for assessing Gender Role Ideology was constructed for the purpose of the study. The scale was designed to elicit simple *Yes/No* responses to ensure acceptability and understandability among people from all social classes. The steps for scale construction were as follows:

Step I: Initially a number of items were constructed with the help of experts in psychology and economics. The items were checked for face validity and edited and a preliminary scale consisting of 15 items was constructed. A value of 1 was assigned to *Yes* response and a value of 0 to *No* response. The items were so constructed that a *Yes* response indicated orthodox gender role ideology. Thus a higher score indicated gender orthodoxy.

Step II: A total of 200 data were extracted from the initial pool of data through stratified random sampling technique. They were administered the preliminary scale and the data were analysed with SPSS 10. Item-total correlations were calculated and items with a corrected item total correlation value below 0.35, were eliminated. Ultimately 8 items were retained. The contribution of each item to the total score is presented in Table A3.1.1.

Table A3.1.1: Item Total Correlation (Corrected) for the 8 Items.

Items of the Gender Role Ideology Scale	*Item Total Correlation (r)*	*Significance*
1. Do you believe that women should not opt for outside employment as far as possible?	0.50	P < 0.01
2. Do you think it is shameful if a wife earns more than her husband?	0.54	P < 0.01
3. Do you think that it is shameful for a man to do work like sweeping the floor or washing vessels?	0.48	P < 0.01
4. Even under conditions of severe financial stress, do you think that there are some jobs that a woman may take up but a man should not (e.g., menial work)?	0.52	P < 0.01

(contd...)

Table A3.1.1 (continued)

Items of the Gender Role Ideology Scale	*Item Total Correlation (r)*	*Significance*
5. If you were to have only one child would you rather have a son?	0.34	P < 0.01
6. Do you think that a man loses respect in the community if his wife or daughter moves about freely outside the home?	0.47	P < 0.01
7. Do you think that a woman or girl who goes out alone after dark is herself to be blamed if she gets molested?	0.47	P < 0.01
8. Do you think that a girl or woman who moves about freely outside the house is most likely to be a 'loose' woman?	0.45	P < 0.01

Step III: The preliminary scale was now converted to the working scale consisting of 8 items. A total of 356 data were again extracted from the initial pool of data through stratified random sampling technique. They were administered the working scale and data were analysed with SPSS 10 for reliability and factorial validity. The results are presented in Tables A3.1.2, A3.1.3 and A3.1.4. The tables indicate an acceptable level of reliability. Principal Components Factor analysis with Varimax rotation elicited two factors—the first one being of 6 items (named 'relative social statuses') and the other one of 2 items (named 'relative job statuses'). The total percentage of variance explained by the two factors was 52.096%.

Table A3.1.2: Alpha and Split Half Reliability (with Spearman Brown correction) for the Gender Role Ideology Scale

	The Gender Role Ideology Scale (final format)
Alpha Reliability	0.78
Split Half Reliability (with Spearman Brown correction)	0.69

Table A3.1.3: Results of Principal Components Factor Analysis with Varimax Rotation (using Kaiser normalization)

Components	*Eigen Values* *Total*	*Rotation Sums of Squared Loadings* *Total*	*% of Variance*	*Cumulative %*
1	3.11	2.28	28.493	28.49
2	1.06	1.89	23.603	52.10
3	0.88	NA		
4	0.81	NA		
5	0.72	NA		
6	0.56	NA		
7	0.46	NA		
8	0.39	NA		

Table A3.1.4: Relative Contribution of each Item to the Factors (Rotated Component Matrix)

Item Numbers (as in Table A3.1.1) with Cue Content	*Factors* 1 *(Relative Social Status)*	2 *(Relative Job Status)*
7. Woman who goes out alone after dark is to be blamed	0.79	1.290E-02
6. Man loses respect if his wife or daughter moves freely	0.67	0.15
8. Woman who moves about freely is likely a 'loose' woman	0.66	0.14
2. Shameful if wife earns more than husband	0.54	0.43
1. Women should not go for outside employment	0.52	0.40
5. Would rather have a son	0.42	0.29
3. Shameful for a man to do work like sweeping the floor	9.289E-02	0.89
4. Some jobs that a woman may take up but a man should not	0.199	0.81

Step IV: A working norm prepared from the same 356 data is presented in Table A3.1.5.

Table A3.1.5: Normative Data (mean and SD) for the Gender Role Ideology Scale

		Total sample (N = 356)	*Male (N = 153)*	*Female (N = 203)*
Total score (8 items)	Mean	3.13	2.92	3.30
	SD	2.37	2.28	2.42
Factor 1 (6 items) (Relative social status)	Mean	2.27	2.13	2.37
	SD	1.82	1.79	1.85
Factor 2 (2 items) (Relative job status)	Mean	0.87	0.80	0.92
	SD	0.88	0.89	0.87

Now the gender role ideology scale was ready for use.

APPENDIX 3.2: SOME RESULTS OF THE MULTIVARIATE ANALYSIS

Variable Chart

Age	*Age*	*age*
Age*2	Age square	age_sq
Education	Illiterate + literate without schooling	Base
	Primary + Up	e11
	Secondary & above	e12
Marital Status	1 Unmarried	Base
	2 Currently Married	m11
	3 Others	m12
Work status	Govt. sector + autonomous + corporate + private	Base
	Self employed + house labour + agriculture + agricultural labour + unemployed	w11
	No need of job	w12
	Student	w13
	House work	w14
Economic Status	1 Very good	Base
	2 Good	es11
	3 Poor	es12
Caste/Religion	SC/ST	Base
	Nair	rl_11
	Ezhava	rl_12
	Syrian Christian + Other Christian	rl_13
	Shia Muslim + Sunni Muslim	rl_14
	Others	rl_15
Region	1 South	Base
	2 Central	rg11
	3 North	rg12
GI total	GI Total – 8 questions	gi8total
Sex	Male	Base
	Female	s1

Equation A3.2.1: Marginal Coefficients (Probit model) Comparison of Men and Women with GHQ Scores as the Dependent Variable

Females			*Males*		
ghq	dF/dx	z	ghq	dF/dx	z
age	0.013	1.91	age	0.01	2.31
age_sq	-0.00	-1.42	age_sq	-0.00	-1.92
e11*	0.03	0.56	e11*	-0.15	-1.93
e12*	-0.08	-1.25	e12*	-0.22	-2.63
m11*	0.00	0.01	m11*	0.03	0.43
m12*	0.13	1.57	m12*	0.01	0.15
w11*	0.01	0.14	w11*	0.04	0.75
w12*	-0.02	-0.2	w12*	0.25	2.8
w13*	-0.23	-2.38	w13*	-0.01	-0.21
w14*	-0.14	-1.84	w14*	-0.00	-0.05
es11*	0.01	0.31	es11*	-0.02	-0.57
es12*	0.07	1.65	es12*	0.03	0.66
rl_11*	-0.04	-0.61	rl_11*	0.10	1.39
rl_12*	0.01	0.28	rl_12*	0.12	1.88
rl_13*	0.04	0.79	rl_13*	0.05	0.78
rl_14*	-0.01	-0.31	rl_14*	0.05	0.73
rl_15*	0.00	0	rl_15*	0.04	0.61
rg11*	-0.04	-1.28	rg11*	-0.04	-1.1
rg12*	-0.08	-2.02	rg12*	-0.02	-0.45
gi8total	0.02	3.63	gi8total	0.02	2.79
obs. P	0.57		obs. P	0.53	
pred. P	0.58		pred. P	0.54	

Number of obs = 1241
LR chi2(20) = 139.06
Prob > chi2 = 0.0000
Log likelihood = -776.52349

Number of obs = 988
LR chi2(20) = 87.42
Prob > chi2 = 0.0000
Log likelihood = -638.19343

Equation A3.2.2: Odds Ratios (Logit model) Comparison of Men and Women with GHQ Scores as the Dependent Variable

Females			*Males*		
ghq	Odds Ratio	z	ghq	Odds Ratio	z
age	1.05	1.91	age	1.07	2.34
age_sq	0.99	-1.43	age_sq	0.99	-1.95
e11	1.13	0.56	e11	0.50	-1.96
e12	0.71	-1.26	e12	0.37	-2.62
m11	1.00	0	m11	1.14	0.45
m12	1.80	1.59	m12	1.06	0.16
w11	1.04	0.11	w11	1.18	0.77
w12	0.90	-0.17	w12	3.32	2.8
w13	0.37	-2.4	w13	0.93	-0.19
w14	0.53	-1.87	w14	0.95	-0.07
es11	1.05	0.29	es11	0.88	-0.64
es12	1.37	1.58	es12	1.14	0.58
rl_11	0.81	-0.68	rl_11	1.57	1.4
rl_12	1.06	0.25	rl_12	1.73	1.91
rl_13	1.20	0.73	rl_13	1.23	0.76
rl_14	0.90	-0.35	rl_14	1.23	0.7
rl_15	1.01	0.03	rl_15	1.20	0.6
rg11	0.81	-1.33	rg11	0.83	-1.08
rg12	0.69	-2.07	rg12	0.91	-0.46
gi8total	1.10	3.65	gi8total	1.09	2.87

Equation A3.2.3: Marginal Coefficients (Probit)
Comparison of GHQ Dummy for Men and Women

Females			*Males*		
ghqd	dF/dx	z	ghqd	dF/dx	z
age	0.01	2.18	age	0.00	1.51
age_sq	-0.00	-1.48	age_sq	-8.8E-05	-1.23
el1*	0.00	0.13	el1*	-0.09	-1.44
el2*	-0.13	-2.39	el2*	-0.12	-1.89
ml1*	-0.01	-0.15	ml1*	-0.01	-0.19
ml2*	0.11	1.3	ml2*	0.019	0.22
wl1*	0.015	0.18	wl1*	0.11	2.27
wl2*	-0.02	-0.25	wl2*	0.27	2.94
wl3*	-0.04	-0.45	wl3*	0.04	0.5
wl4*	-0.05	-0.65	wl4*	0.33	1.89
esl1*	-0.02	-0.53	esl1*	0.03	0.88
esl2*	0.06	1.33	esl2*	0.10	2.09
rl_l1*	-0.04	-0.66	rl_l1*	0.04	0.55
rl_l2*	-0.02	-0.51	rl_l2*	0.06	1.02
rl_l3*	0.00	0.1	rl_l3*	0.00	0.13
rl_l4*	-0.06	-1.16	rl_l4*	-0.02	-0.46
rl_l5*	-0.02	-0.33	rl_l5*	-0.03	-0.6
rgl1*	-0.05	-1.51	rgl1*	0.02	0.56
rgl2*	-0.05	-1.38	rgl2*	0.02	0.62
gi8total	0.02	3.19	gi8total	0.03	4.42
obs. P	0.38		obs. P	0.29	
pred. P	0.37		pred. P	0.28	

Number of obs = 1241
LR chi2(20) = 137.33
Prob > chi2 = 0.0000
Log likelihood = -756.12913

Number of obs = 988
LR chi2(20) = 87.38
Prob > chi2 = 0.0000
Log likelihood = -556.07076

Equation A3.2.4: Marginal Coefficients (Probit)
Comparison of SUBI Dummy for Men and Women

Females			*Males*		
subid	dF/dx	z	subid	dF/dx	z
age	-0.00	-0.11	age	0.00	1.07
age_sq	3.84E-05	0.48	age_sq	-7.5E-05	-0.92
e11*	-0.10	-1.94	e11*	-0.13	-1.63
e12*	-0.22	-3.32	e12*	-0.25	-2.83
m11*	0.00	0	m11*	0.08	1.17
m12*	0.08	1.08	m12*	0.12	1.41
w11*	0.12	1.61	w11*	0.21	3.84
w12*	-0.18	-1.51	w12*	0.22	2.74
w13*	-0.04	-0.52	w13*	0.08	1.12
w14*	0.02	0.39	w14*	0.16	0.98
es11*	0.05	1.36	es11*	0.13	2.87
es12*	0.17	4.15	es12*	0.11	2.19
rl_11*	-0.04	-0.64	rl_11*	-0.04	-0.63
rl_12*	-0.03	-0.63	rl_12*	-0.00	-0.1
rl_13*	-0.02	-0.36	rl_13*	-0.06	-0.91
rl_14*	-0.10	-1.58	rl_14*	-0.07	-1.01
rl_15*	-0.04	-0.65	rl_15*	-0.01	-0.26
rg11*	-0.02	-0.67	rg11*	0.01	0.32
rg12*	0.00	0.18	rg12*	0.04	1.09
gi8total	0.02	3.25	gi8total	0.01	2.4

Number of obs = 1241
LR chi2(20) = 124.69
Prob > chi2 = 0.0000
Log likelihood = -742.15321

Number of obs = 988
LR chi2(20) = 109.46
Prob > chi2 = 0.0000
Log likelihood = -613.60912

Equation A3.2.5
Probit and Logit Analysis for the Combined (M+F) Sample for Dichotomized MH indicators: GHQD and SUBID

Odds Ratios GHQD			*Odds Ratios with SUBID*		
ghqd	Odds Ratio	z	subid	Odds Ratio	z
age	1.06	2.76	age	1.01	0.58
age_sq	0.99	-2.02	age_sq	0.99	-0.17
e11	0.86	-0.84	e11	0.60	-2.33
e12	0.54	-3	e12	0.38	-4.06
m11	0.92	-0.33	m11	1.24	1.05
m12	1.40	1.19	m12	1.72	2.08
w11	1.51	1.94	w11	2.23	4.23
w12	1.98	2.19	w12	1.46	1.21
w13	1.12	0.4	w13	1.20	0.76
w14	1.26	1.04	w14	1.47	1.85
es11	0.99	-0.06	es11	1.44	2.89
es12	1.42	2.26	es12	1.99	4.58
rl_11	0.96	-0.15	rl_11	0.81	-0.87
rl_12	1.08	0.41	rl_12	0.92	-0.38
rl_13	1.056	0.29	rl_13	0.86	-0.75
rl_14	0.79	-1.14	rl_14	0.69	-1.77
rl_15	0.87	-0.63	rl_15	0.88	-0.56
rg11	0.90	-0.87	rg11	0.97	-0.21
rg12	0.90	-0.75	rg12	1.12	0.91
s1	1.46	2.63	s1	1.39	2.35
gi8total	1.11	5.23	gi8total	1.08	3.91

Number of obs = 2229	Number of obs = 2229
LR chi2(21) = 219.68	LR chi2(21) = 215.32
Prob > chi2 = 0.0000	Prob > chi2 = 0.0000
Log likelihood = -1323.7149	Log likelihood = -1369.0538

REFERENCES

Adelmann, P., 1994, 'Multiple Roles and Psychological Well-being in a National Sample of Older Adults', *Journal of Gerontology*, 49, pp. 277–85.

Basu, J., 2003, 'Risk Factors, Prevention and Culture-compliant Intervention for Some Psychiatric Disorders prevalent among Women', Report submitted to Kolkata: DST.

Basu, S., 2004, 'A Study of Gender Role Stereotypes of College Students in Relation to some Mental Health Variables', unpublished Ph.D. thesis, Calcutta: Calcutta University.

Belk, S.S. and Snell, W.E., 1989, 'Stereotypic Beliefs about Women as Moderators of Stress-Distress Relationships', *Journal of Clinical Psychology*, 45, pp. 665–72.

Bolger, N., DeLongis, A., Kessler, R.C. and Schilling, E.A., 1989, 'Effects of Daily Stress on Negative Mood', *Journal of Personality and Social Psychology*, 57, pp. 808–18.

Busfield, J., 1996, *Men, Women and Madness*, Houndsmills, Hampshire: Macmillan Press.

Cameron, J.E. and Lalonde, R.N., 2001, 'Social Identification and Gender-related Ideology in Women and Men', *British Journal of Social Psychology*, 40, pp. 59–77.

Cleary, P.D. and Mechanic, D., 1983, 'Sex Differences in Psychological Distress among Married People', *Journal of Health and Social Behavior*, 24, pp. 111–21.

Davar, B., 1999, *Mental Health of Indian Women: A Feminist Agenda*, New Delhi: Sage Publications.

Diener, E., Suh, E.M., Lucas, R.E. and Smith, H., 1997, 'Subjective Well-being: Three Decades of Progress 1967–1997', Illinois: University of Illinois.

Goldberg, D.P. and Hiller, V.E., 1979, 'A Scaled Version of the General Health Questionnaire', *Psychological Medicine*, 9, pp. 139–46.

Gove, W.R., 1979, 'Sex Differences in the Epidemiology of Mental Disorders: Evidence and Explanations', E. S. Gomberg and V. Franks (eds.), *Gender and Disordered Behavior: Sex Differences in Psychopathology*, New York: Brunner/Mazel, pp. 23–68.

Helson, R., Elliot, T. and Leigh, J., 1990, 'Number and Quality of Roles', *Psychological of Women Quarterly*, 14, pp. 83–101.

Kuiper, N.A. and Dance, K.A., 1994, 'Dysfunctional Attitudes, Roles, Stress Evaluations, and Psychological Well being', *Journal of Research in Personality*, 28, pp. 245–62.

Landrine, H., Klonoff, E.A., Gibbs, J., Manning, V. and Lund, M., 1995, 'Physical and Psychiatric Correlates of Gender Discrimination: An Application of the Schedule of Sexist Incidents', *Psychology of Women Quarterly*, 19, pp. 473–92.

Lorber, J., 1997, *Gender and the Social Construction of Illness*, New Delhi: Sage Publications.

Malik, S., 1993, 'Women and Mental Health', Presidential address in the 45th Annual Conference of the Indian Psychiatric Society, Lucknow.

McIntyre, S. and Hunt, K., 1997, 'Socio-economic Position, Gender and Health', *Journal of Health Psychology*, 2, pp. 315–34.

Mohamed, E., Rajan, S.I., Kumar, Anil K. and Mohammed, P.M. Saidu, 2002, 'Gender and Mental Health in Kerala', Report of the Kerala Mental Health Survey (KMHS), submitted to the Gender Network, New Delhi: Institute of Social Studies Trust.

Mukhopadhyay, Swapna, 2003, 'What is new about "Gender Bias"?', Swapna Mukhopadhyay and Ratna Sudarshan (eds.), *Tracking Gender Development: Continuity and Change in South Asia*, New Delhi: Kali for Women.

Pearlin, L.I., 1975, 'Sex Roles and Depression', N. Datan and L.H. Ginsberg (eds.), *Life-span Developmental Psychology: Normative Life Crises*, New York: Academic Press, pp. 191–207.

Ratner, P. A., 1993, 'The Incidence of Wife Abuse and Mental Health Status in Abused Wives in Edmonton, Alberta', *Canada Journal of Public Health*, 83, pp. 246–9.

Ruble, D.N., Greulich, F., Pomerantz, E.M. and Gochberg, B., 1993, 'The Role of Gender-related Processes in the Development of Sex Differences in Self-evaluation and Depression', *Special Issue: Toward a New Psychobiology of Depression in Women, Journal of Affective Disorders*, 29, pp. 97–128.

Russo, N.F., 1990, 'Overview: Forging Research Priorities for Women's Mental Health', *American Psychologist*, 45, pp. 368–73.

Sell, H. and Nagpal, R., 1992, 'Assessment of Subjective Well being', World Health Organization, Regional office for South East Asia, New Delhi.

Sugarman, D. and Frankel, S.L., 1996, 'Patriarchal Ideology and Wife-assault: A Meta-analytic Review', *Journal of Family Violence*, 11, pp. 13–40.

Weissman, M.M., Bland, R., Joyce, P.R., Newman, S., Wells, J.E. and Wittchen, H., 1993, 'Sex Differences in Rates of Depression: Cross-national Perspectives', *Journal of Affective Disorders*, 29, pp. 77–84.

World Health Organization Report 2000, 'Women's Mental Health: An Evidence based Review', Mental Health Determinants and Populations, Department of Mental Health and Substance Dependence, Geneva.

Zachariah, K.C., Mathew, E.T. and Rajan, S.I., 2003, *Dynamics of Migration in Kerala: Dimensions, Differentials and Consequences*, New Delhi: Orient Longman.

chapter four

Re-forming Women in Malayalee Modernity

A Historical Overview

J. Devika and Avanti Mukherjee

INTRODUCTION

A quick look at the contemporary literature of early twentieth century social reforms in Kerala will convince us of its striking difference from the experience of social reform elsewhere (Kodoth 2001).[1] Unlike elsewhere in India (Chatterjee 1989; Sarkar 1996; O'Hanlon 2000), here we find stronger state intervention[2] and ample presence of community-subjects who actively demanded change in social and family practices. Community movements actively sought state legislation; they also sought to create subjects capable of demanding reform through a variety of ways (Awaya 1996; Velayudhan 1999; Kodoth 2001).

The presence of strong 'community movements'[3] that sought to transform traditional jatis into modern communities was characteristic

[1]For a more detailed discussion on the subject from a gender perspective, see Devika 2007.

[2]In Travancore, the state intervened in the community practices early enough as evidenced by Rani Satu Parvaty Bai's proclamation regulating dowry among the Malayala brahmins in 1822–3. See Nair and Pushpa 1992: 181–2.

[3]I use the term 'community movements' in lieu of other, perhaps more familiar notions like 'caste associations' to avoid projecting them as liberal public associations, and to bring in the following nuances evident in this phenomenon in Kerala. Community movements not only integrated members of particular castes into associations organized on modern lines and oriented towards the nascent modern public sphere, but also in a strong sense, shaped modern community subjects as bearers of a certain imagined 'tradition' and common values ascribed

of Malayalee social reform (Gopalakrishnan 1994). Indeed, in the twentieth century, community reformism and interests were to have an appeal that neither nationalism nor communism could ignore (Menon 1972, 1994). Shaped by such conditions as the modernization of the government in Travancore and Cochin, the spreading cash economy, a nascent public sphere, missionary presence and so on, community movements worked to alter traditional jati inequalities, reform marriage and family structures, and help members acquire modern education to ensure the presence of the community in the new fields being opened up in Malayalee modernity. Above all, the project of shaping the modern governable individual was common to all of them (Devika 2006).

Intimations of new forms of the patriarchal order were present in the earliest Malayalee reformist writing. Indeed, recent work by women's historians in Kerala have questioned the assumption that patriarchy in Kerala is largely a vestige of undesirable pre-modern social practices and beliefs, dominant in popular discourse around the 'Kerala model', as well as in historical writings about the late nineteenth-early twentieth-century Kerala. They have sought to identify new forms of patriarchal power and institutions that were shaped precisely in and through the processes that have been identified as central to Kerala's social development (Awaya 1996; Velayudhan 1999; Kodoth 2001; Zachariah and Devika 2007). For instance, early reformers, ranging from missionaries to community movements, sought to redo Malayalee family and marriage practices along the lines of what they perceived to be the ideal high-Hindu form. This form was often perceived as being simultaneously 'Indian' and 'modern'.

It has been argued that this paved the way for a specific form of patriarchy, 'conjugal patriarchy', in twentieth-century Malayalee society (Kodoth 2006). Likewise, modern education was important as the major instrument in shaping modern public-oriented male subjects and modern domestic-oriented female subjects, who were thereby, implicated in shaping new hierarchies. This seems to have produced new forms of power, claiming to be specifically 'feminine', which however, was closely implicated in the creation of new gender hierarchies (Devika 2007).

---

to the community. Thus participants in community movements were not simply born into it, or associating as individuals, in the liberal sense, for common ends; they were directly involved in shaping a modern community projected into the future, from the pre-exexisting more fragmented caste groups. Cf, Devika 2007.

Malayalee reformism has had an extraordinarily long innings, spanning till the end of the twentieth century (Devika 2006a). Among the many groups targeted, women were prominent as evident for instance, from the nineteenth century missionary novel set in Travancore, *The Slayer Slain* (1877) (Collins 1990). It was claimed that reformed women would pass on modern ideals and practices to the family; an idea that waxed stronger with time (for instance, Mateer 1991; Krishnan 1958; Devika 2006). Modern gender attained an unprecedented centrality in reformist visions of an ideal society. Common codes of gendered conduct were weakly operative across caste groupings in traditional Malayalee society (Bhaskaranunny 1988) and reformers laid out precisely these in shaping modern subjectivities. The recognition that the ideology of modern gender fostered non-reciprocal power relations between the sexes may be crucial to the understanding of Kerala's 'gender paradox' (Erwer 2003).

In the first section of this chapter, we examine how the ideology gender equality has historically shaped several fields of social development, which may explain at least partially, the ambiguous 'liberation' of Malayalee women. This sets the background for a closer look at the present in the subsequent section.

EDUCATION

The justification for female education in Malayalee society fell squarely within the nineteenth-century colonial project of 'civilizing the natives'. This was also a project of 'properly gendering' them for instance, in James Mill's *The History of British India* (1817). This coincided with the rise of the 'social' in the West, as part of managing the 'unruly masses' unleashed by the Industrial Revolution. The category 'women' was reconstructed towards an expanded 'domestic' identity, resulting in the view that female education would benefit 'society' as a whole, and not just lead to 'the good of men' or 'women's spiritual redemption' (Riley 1995).

Late nineteenth- early twentieth-century arguments for female education linked it to the emergent institution of the modern, moral home, imagining the educated woman to be its fulcrum. Matrilineal families, it seemed, made women indolent and promiscuous—as argued by the late nineteenth-century Malayalam novel *Meenakshi* (Nair 1985) while prevailing patrilineal forms seemed to enslave them, as argued by the well-known Malayala Brahmin reformer, V.T. Bhattatiripad (1988). In contrast, the educated woman would realize her full 'gendered potential' by overseeing the disciplining of individuals and the rational utilization of materials within the domestic. While such capacity seemed 'inherently' present in women, it seemed necessary to refine it through training, or 'female education'. Thus 'female education' referred to was not just the acquisition of literacy, but also to a set of gendered attitudes and skills.[4]

This idea became popular among the modern-educated new elite in Kerala by the turn of the nineteenth century. Late nineteenth-century Malayalam novels, for instance, *Indulekha* (1889) were vocal about this (Menon 1989). The *Gazetteer of Travancore* (1891) proudly highlighted the higher levels of female literacy as an illustration of the 'enlightened' condition of Travancore.[5] State support for female education was actively forthcoming carrying forward the already present aspects of 'enlightened attitudes'. Women in both matrilineal and patrilineal communities in Kerala often received training and sometimes, even a traditional scholarly education. Besides in the states of Travancore and Cochin, community movements promoted female education (Jeffrey 2003). In 1898, 19 per cent of all girls of the primary age group in Travancore and 14 per cent in Cochin were going to school. By the late 1950s, 87 per cent of the girls of this age group in Kerala were in school (Jeffrey 2003: 55).

Early arguments for female education claimed that educated women influenced society powerfully through adequate performance of motherly and housewifely roles. In these, the woman's contribution to society was crucial, but more or less indirect (Amma 1924–5). However, this idea gained in importance in the early decades of the twentieth century. Many first-generation modern educated women argued that female education should prepare women not just for active domestic life but also for social management. Many 'womanly' capacities, it was claimed, were necessary in a society run on modern lines. For instance, women's supposedly natural capacity for disciplining the young through love was found to have application in the modern

[4]This persisted long: in 1945, resolutions favouring education for women that would make them good home makers were still being discussed in the Travancore Sree Mulam Popular Assembly. See, M.R.Ramakrishna Pillai put forth a Resolution (No. 56), 9 August 1945, *Proceedings of the Shree Mulam Popular Assembly* Vol. XXVI, 1946, 1277–80.

[5]This was an important element in V. Nagam Aiya's representation of Travancore as the ideal Hindu kingdom in his *Report of the Census of Travancore* (1891), noticed and commented on by reviewers. See quote from such a review in his biography written by 'An Old School Fellow and Friend', 1911: 36.

school; their alleged greater capacity for caring labour seemed to be in need in the hospital; their putative capacity for persuasion was found necessary for the smooth running of modern political institutions (Devika 2006).

What is interesting about these arguments is that even while they associate reason with male and emotion with female, they do concede in large measure a capacity for rational deliberation to women. In other words, such education did allow female individuation as a possible outcome. However, this possibility was to be limited and given a 'domestic' shape through self-sacrificial domestic ideologies. We, therefore, find that female education in early twentieth-century Malayalee society did produce a set of powerful women intellectuals and professionals who engaged their male contemporaries in rational debate (Devika 2005a). But sacrificial domestic ideologies also gained in reach, often through these very women-intellectuals. The project of shaping the ideal female subjectivity extended beyond schools, a fact little noticed in the histories of education in Kerala. While school education offered the possibility of individuation and independence through employment, other non-formal educative institutions such as the *streesamajam* (the women's association) promoted by reformist organizations, schools and churches actively propagated domestic ideologies (Devika 1998). Early twentieth-century women's magazines in Malayalam were another site in which these two tendencies are equally present, often at odds with each other (Velayudhan 1994).

However, in the early twentieth century these ideas were still limited to the modern educated new elite. Women in agricultural and artisan work, women workers in modern industries and plantations (Rammohan 1996:86) were largely outside their reach. Expanding literacy was one way in which these ideals reached the working classes; however, they remained largely irrelevant for the majority of working class women. But modern gender did begin to structure working-class lives by the mid twentieth-century through other routes, which are equally important. Anna Lindberg has for instance, brilliantly documented the manner in which bureaucrats, factory owners and trade unions participated equally in firmly institutionalizing the male breadwinner norm in wage-fixing agreements of the 1950s and thereby, pushed women workers into the status of secondary earners. This, she observes, has had important material consequences for women and families; but more crucially, it has worked to strongly shape women's own perceptions of work and entrench gendered divisions of labour within the factory (Lindberg 2001).

Gender stereotyping has continued to persist in post-independence times in the field of education in Kerala, despite the fact that both girls and boys are equally educated (Kodoth and Eapen 2005). The double expectation imposed on contemporary Kerala girls is, however, of concern. While they are expected to perform as well as the boys at school or college, the additional burden of having to conform to the norms of femininity is unmistakable. This has produced a contradictory situation, particularly prominent under present circumstances.

Young girls have to learn to limit the processes of individuation, by a complex combination of a more thorough breakdown of the traditional caste system on the one hand and modern education on the other. They have to tailor them strictly to the requirements, economic and other, of the modern family. These pressures manifest themselves among the poor in Kerala as well. Ethnography among the children of fisher folk in Kerala has revealed that little girls do perceive sharply, the difference between work and education, and the housework they alone have to do, and how the forced negotiation between the two, generates tension (Niuewenhuys 1999: 6).

EMPLOYMENT

Employment for women did not figure initially on the agenda of the reforming agencies. Initially, women-agents were found necessary to reach other women as targets—thus there were arguments in the 1890s, for female smallpox vaccinators, female teachers, trained midwives and missionary 'bible women' (*Report of the Administration of Travancore* 1869–70: 112; Haggis 2000). Indeed women found employment initially precisely in such capacities (*Report of the Administration of Travancore* 1868–69: 69; 1869–70:112; Nair 1947).

The number of women seeking employment went up decisively in the 1930s and 1940s, especially in Travancore and Kochi.[6] Modern educated women sought paid employment in Travancore, as the Statham Committee's report on educational reform noted; the authors opined that women viewed education mainly as a means for securing employment (*Report of the Travancore Educational Reforms Committee* 1933: 262–3). The 1931 Census Report of Travancore remarked that employed women refrained from getting married, and predicted

[6]In 1929, there were 238 female students in the colleges of Tiruvitamkoor.(Pillai (1940), 1996: 695). The *Unemployment Enquiry Committee Report of Travancore* (1928), reported that about 450 women were earning qualifications for employment yearly in Travancore (*Malayala Manorama, MM* from now, 6 July 1928).

that this would lead to a fall in marriages (*Census of India 1931, Travancore:* 170).

However, this was not to be so. Certainly, women striving for mobility often sought employment—many autobiographies testify to this (for instance, Devi 2004). However, mounting economic difficulties of families may have also pushed many women into the job market. Population growth rates in Travancore and Cochin increased substantially between 1901–41 implying larger families to support (Panikar and Soman 1984: 35–6). Economic crises, changing agrarian relations and legislation abolishing the impartibility of joint family properties exacerbated the difficulties of families (Saradamoni 1999; Velayudhan 1999). Also important are changes in the institution of marriage like the emergence of dowry in Nair and Ezhava marriages and changing dowry practices among Syrian Christians.[7] These pressures could have pushed women from the traditional elite in which girls did study and in which the stigma on women's economic contribution was less pronounced, to actively seek education and employment without necessarily seeking autonomy, as several autobiographies and literary accounts from this period testify (for instance, Devi 2004; Nair 1947; Amma, Kalyani 1968).

Community movements and leaders like the Nair leader Mannath Padmanabhan and E.M.S Nambutiripad appealed to their womenfolk to engage in gainful work around the home to bolster the finances of the new family (Amma, Meenakshi 2005 (1924); Pillai 1977; Nambutiripad 1945). Tensions remained though community movements expressed considerable pride at the achievements of the women in employment—recognizing it mainly as the achievement of the community (Devika 1998). It was in the 1920s and 1930s that community movements passionately pursued their gender agenda focused on creating the new domestic domain and installing women as the managers of this space. Their annual conferences, many a time presided by women-achievers of the community, most often exhorted women to become able home-managers—despite dissonant voices (for instance, Chacko 2005 [1927]). Opinions about women's employment were divided, though many male reformers were sympathetic to

[7] The dissolution of matriliny opened fewer possibilities for women than men, yet it forced choices on them as well (Jeffrey, 2003, 49). The 1931 census report of Travancore clearly mentions the direct and indirect rise of dowry among matrilineal groups. See, *Census of India 1931, Travancore*—Part 1 Vol. XXVIII, 162. See, also Amma, K. Padmavaty 2005 (1924); Kodoth 2002.

women's aspirations for employment. Indeed, the consensus that seemed to have emerged was that women could indeed engage in paid work outside the home provided these occupations were 'womanly', and such employment added to the security and upward mobility of the family.

Justifications of women's paid work are to be found, most vociferously of all, in the writings of the first generation of educated women, Kerala's 'first-generation feminists' (Devika 2005a). For them, the challenge of women's freedom was that of expanding women's social space without endangering their 'womanly' identity. Therefore they sought to argue for the presence of women in areas of the public where the putatively gendered qualities of women seemed urgently required. Therefore, teaching, nursing, caregiving professions, as well as such niches within 'male' professions as the police and law, were generally seen as suitable for women.[8]

The tension between the employed woman's different commitments was another theme that echoed through the debates about women's employment in the early twentieth-century Malayalee public sphere. Right from the early-twentieth century, employed women protested against moves to restrict government employment to unmarried women on the grounds that married women had divided loyalties (Nair 1947; Chandy 2005 [1929]). This is a history that was carried into the early 1950s, which again reflects the terms on which women entered employment in Kerala.[9]

The continuously falling rates of work participation of women in Kerala have received some attention now (Kumar 1994; Kodoth and Eapen 2005). However, the fact that Kerala has one of the highest rates of female unemployment in India implies that there are women actively seeking work (Kodoth and Eapen 2005). It may be claimed now that this is an effect of the negotiation that women often make between their roles in the home and the work place, such that the former tends to set the terms under which the latter may be sought.

[8]Even women who entered professions that were considered masculine were portrayed as somehow bringing femininity into them. See for instance, the Malayalam newspaper *Matrubhumi* 's depiction of Justice Anna Chandy as a 'Womanly legal authority' in its editorial, 'Justice Anna Chandy', 5 April 1967. Indeed she preferred such representation. See, *MM*, 23 November 1964: 1.

[9]The branch of the All-India Women's Conference met at Cochin and passed a resolution on 6 September 1951 against the rule that nurses should remain unmarried, requesting the Tiru-Kochi government to do away with this rule, *MM*, 7 September 1951.

Hence, 'respectable' work closer to the home is preferred (Eapen 1992; Devi 2002). Strong negative connotations attached to women doing manual work are also applicable to Kerala, as also the association with straitened circumstances (Chasin 1990:5; Uyl 1995:138; Osella and Osella 2000:41; Lindberg 2001). Also, women have a tendency to move out of the workforce once the family has moved up to a certain level in the social ladder, through male occupational mobility and migration. Wives of migrants to the Gulf, though more educated on an average than the general female population, were largely housewives, and when working, were better represented in government employment alone (Zachariah et al. 2004) than the average woman.

Recent studies show that women workers who migrate out of the country and earn a substantial amount, use their financial clout to create more space for themselves within the male dominated families without challenging its terms radically. These gains stay well within the new kind of family structure which was not traditional in the old sense of the term but were not really emancipatory either.

Marriage remained the major life-goal of these women (George 1999: Gallo 2005). Also, irrespective of whatever home-centred gains women may have made in public, they were expected to conform to the accepted manner and deportment of femininity. This is particularly marked among Mappila women who have only recently begun to enter higher education in large numbers. A recent study notes that the practice of veiling has spread among Mappila college-going women, is an effort to create a 'decent' and feminine public dress for Muslim women (Jong 2004: 9).

Work opportunities in agriculture especially paddy cultivation, cashew and coir industry, handlooms, which employed women in large numbers, have been shrinking (Kannan 2005). Some women have been absorbed by the expanding construction and quarry works. At the other end, women are still a minority in the service sector, for instance, in software, public administration and banking, and are often stuck at the lower end of both pay scales and positions of authority (Kannan 2005). Liberalization with its concomitant structural shifts in the economy has led to service-sector based growth, which has attracted women to work with low pay and poor working conditions, but has 'respectability'. Recent government efforts to generate employment, like the state's poverty eradication mission, the, Kudumbashree has also ensured 'respectability', which may be counted as a key reason for its wide acceptance (Thampi and Devika 2005).

HEALTH

Health has been an area in which the achievement of gender parity in Kerala appeared to have been beyond dispute. The striking reductions achieved in maternal and infant mortality has been an important factor for Kerala's image of being a 'model' state (Jeffrey 2003). The expansion of healthcare services, high female literacy and widespread acceptance of contraception have been identified as major factors responsible for Kerala being held up as being exemplary. Though some have, in recent times, questioned the decline of sex ratio in Kerala (Rajan et al. 2000), women's health continues to be noted as an exceptional achievement in Kerala's development.

Several qualifiers, however, seem to be necessary. First, it needs to be recognized that the health status of women of marginal groups in Kerala is far from satisfactory (see Pushpangadan and Murugan 2000). Some recent micro-studies reveal that the nutritional status of women, especially young women in certain districts is far from being adequate (Begum 2001). And most importantly, what the dominant view fails to see is that while the above-mentioned factors are instrumental in creating several desirable developmental outcomes, not one of these need necessarily lead to the unseating of gender discriminating norms. The modernization of childbirth was perceived to be of prime importance for social and family welfare. This led to an early identification of women's health with maternal health in Kerala. Both the state and reform organizations, often through the network of women's associations, made strenuous efforts to educate women in good healthcare practices while expanding medical facilities. This has never challenged the identification of female bodies as being the instruments of serving the well-being of patrifocal families. This is especially evident in the way birth control in Kerala has primarily served to secure the interests of families and the state, and hardly the women themselves. Birth control became acceptable in Kerala only when it was firmly tied to the interests of the family. Indeed, the discourse of family planning from the late 1950s to the 1980s illustrates the extent to which contraception was projected as an instrument of serving the family's strategy for survival and upward mobility, not the expansion of women's life-choices (Devika 2005b). These conclusions remain unaffected by the fact that researchers have often noticed women themselves taking the lead to opt for sterilization (for instance, Gulati 1983: 35). This speaks of the choices women have, and of the specific but limited agency they possess.

The 'feminization of contraception' in Kerala, which began around the 1970s has by now, attained alarming proportions.[10] The medicalization of women's bodies seems to have grown apace alongside the expansion of private healthcare, judging from the rate at which caesarian sections in childbirth are growing (Misra and Ramanathan 2001). The large number of abortions taking place seems to indicate that unwanted pregnancies are rather frequent (Jayashree 2005). Also widespread availability of contraception does not mean that the best options are chosen. A study done in a suburban area in Thiruvananthapuram revealed that 60 per cent of the surveyed group never used a condom; of the remaining 40 per cent, the majority used it only as a temporary method. Indeed, even now, safe sex, contraceptive choices or sexual or reproductive health are still matters, not fully public.[11]

A crucial consequence of the identification of maternal health as the primary component of women's health was that other aspects of women's health have received relatively less attention—so also have morbidity and mental health. Such emergent issues are only beginning to be discussed now in Malayalee society (Menon 2003; Soman 2004: 28). New developments arising from social change in the late twentieth-century, such as an alarming dip in the age of marriage of girls in the Malappuram district, have been reported (Basheer 2004). Some recent research seems to indicate that a substantial section of even poor women in Kerala are overweight (Soman 2004: 27–8).[12]

Three things seem to be evident from the above discussion. One, while the concern for women's health (or 'maternal health') has yielded undeniable and visible gains for dominant sections of Malayalee society, it has been largely driven by concern regarding familial and larger 'societal' well being. Secondly, tied as it was to concerns of family

[10]While 1545 vasectomies were conducted in Kerala in 2000–01, 149,498 tubectomies were done; in 1999–2000, the corresponding figures were 653 and 153,515. See tables C 3.2; C 3.3, *Family Welfare Year Book 2001 2003*.

[11]Ibid; also in their report on gender in the decentralization process in Kerala, Aleyamma Vijayan and J. Sandhya mention an incident in which a proposal for sanitary napkin production was booed out of the panchayats as 'indecent', Vijayan and Sandhya 2004: 47. Very recently, the shadow of AIDS has led to the promotion of sex education in schools, though open discussion of women's contraceptive choices or safe sex is still forbidden or highly biased against women's choice.

[12]High levels of tapioca consumption in poor Malayalee households by women, leaving the better food (rice, fish, and vegetables) for other family members, may be one likely reason.

well-being, the voluntary acceptance of contraception in Kerala, while it has reduced women's fertility, has still not facilitated substantial control by women of their bodies, or the expansion of their contraceptive choices. Further, emergent problems in women's health are only beginning to be perceived as serious issues.

POLITICS

Politics was conceived early enough as an exclusively male domain in Kerala and this continues to be the case to this day.[13] However, in early modern political institutions, women had an early entry. They were granted the right to vote for the Shree Mulam Popular Assembly in Travancore in 1919, and became eligible to sit in the House, and were granted equal rights in voting and Membership of the Legislative Council in 1922 (Menon 1972: 62–3). Dr Mary Poonnen Lukose, was made member of the Travancore Legislative Council in 1924, in her capacity as Head of the Medical Department; others like Tottaikkattu Madhavi Amma, Elizabeth Kuruvila and Gauri Pavitran were nominated as women representatives in the legislatures of Travancore and Cochin. In the late 1930s, for the first time a woman legislator, T. Narayani Amma successfully introduced and piloted a legislation in the history of the Shree Mulam Popular Assembly.[14] The practical difficulties, however, seemed quite formidable. Anna Chandy, the first woman to obtain a law degree in Kerala, fought the elections in Travancore in 1931, and faced considerable animosity. When she complained of unfair campaign tactics, the *Malayalarajyam* newspaper published an even more vituperative response.[15]

Besides, by the 1920s and 1930s, there were two significant developments. First, the first generation of modern educated women was demanding at least the partial recognition of 'women' as a group

[13]The levels of female membership in the left political parties CPI (M) and CPI are lower than 10 per cent. The present legislative assembly only 8 women members out of the total of 140, while the former assembly (1996–2001) had just 13 women members. In trade unions too, the situation is dismal: for instance, 6 per cent female leadership despite women constituting 80 per cent of all members characterizes the teachers union. In the state bureaucracy, there are 21 women IAS officers in a total of 178 and 2 women IPS officers out of 116.

[14]The Travancore Child Marriage Restraint Act, passed on 27 January 1940 *The Proceedings of Travancore Shree Mulam Assembly*, Vol. XV, 449. On the same day, she introduced the Travancore Anti-Dowry Bill.

[15]See Editorial, *Nazrani Deepika*, 16 June 1931.

having specific political interests and second, they were beginning to participate in the national and leftist political movements. In Travancore and Cochin in particular, first generation feminists campaigned on behalf of women for job reservations, representation in the legislative bodies and the removal of unfair restrictions on women seeking paid work (Devika 2005a). By the end of the 1940s, however, this generation went into a decline. The reasons for this have yet to be investigated; however, this seems to be part of a national pattern (Forbes 2000). Those who articulated women's politics seemed to have been unable to forge effective alliances with women who were working in the national and left movements, who often found the position of the former unbearably elitist. In Kerala, even in the 1930s, proponents of communal representation had been among the staunchest opponents of the first-generation feminists' demand for gender representation.[16] In the post-independence legislatures, the nominated female representative who represented women as a constituency did not of course exist; and the task of representing women largely fell to elected women members of political parties.

In Malabar, many educated, upper-caste women inspired by Gandhi's privileging of the 'feminine' in *satyagraha,* participated in the Civil Disobedience movement and in Gandhian constructive work (Menon 1972: 172–265). However, the career of Akkamma Varkey who was a prominent figure in Travancore during the struggle against the Dewan in 1938, perhaps reveals how eminent women-politicians in the Congress were gradually marginalized (Jeffrey 2003). After independence, the Congress in Kerala did little to encourage women-politicians, despite appeals in the national scene from leaders like Nehru. Kumbalattu Sanku Pillai, president of the Tiru-Kochi Congress Committee, justified the abysmally low number of women in the Congress candidates' list, claiming that politics was not 'suitable' for women and that Malayalee women having property rights, were 'Empresses of the Home' and did not wish to enter politics,[17] a few prominent women did protest, but there were certainly no outcry.[18] Later in 1958, women—both of the landed elite and of the utterly

[16]For instance the stance taken by the well-known progressive Ezhava reformer Sahodaran K. Ayyappan, in the debate around the Child Marriage Restraint Act in Kochi, *Cochin Legislative Council Proceedings* vol. IV, 1940: 1439.

[17]See statements in *Nazrani Deepika,* 29 October 1951; 19 November 1951.

[18]See statements by A.V. Kuttimalu Amma (*Nazrani Deepika,* 3 November 1951, 5) and Mariakutty John, *Nazrani Deepika,* 8 January 1952, 2; Akkamma Cheriyan, quoted by Jeffery, 2003, 255.

poor fisher folk—were mobilized by communal forces amply supported by the Congress, in militant protests against Kerala's first elected Communist Ministry in the so-called 'Liberation Struggle' (Gopalakrishnan 1987). Despite all the praise for women from the conservative press and leaders like Indira Gandhi, they were warmly congratulated and then gently made to return to the confines of domesticity or apolitical 'social work'.[19]

Working class women began to organize in the 1930s. Struggles by women agricultural workers were beginning to gain strength in the 1930s and the Ambalappuzha Taluk Kayarupiri Tozhilali Sangham, was formed in the 1930s (Devayani 1995). Later in the 1940s, the communist movement, especially under the labour unions organized large numbers of women workers. The Tiruvitamkoor Coir Factory Workers' Union organized women workers in their own factory committees, conducting study classes and camps, and agitating on many issues like arbitrary dismissal from work, unequal wages and maternity benefits (Rammohan 1996: 158–9). The Ambalapuzha Taluk Mahila Sangham was formed as the nucleus of the communist party's women's wing, in 1943 (Velayudhan 1999a: 508). It grew in strength until 1946, when it was banned along with all other mass organizations with the Punnapra-Vayalar uprising. But despite the presence of dedicated full-time activists like K. Meenakshi, and the massive participation of women workers in trade union agitation, observers have noted that women rarely occupied positions of importance in trade union leadership. This situation has not changed. As a study of Kerala's highly successful workers' co-operative, the Dinesh Beedi, pointed out, 60 per cent of the workers of the co-operative were women but they were not present in the Central Society Director Board, or the pension and welfare committees (Issac et al. 1998: 21). The Left did not seem to be more promising in inducting more women into formal politics, even in its heydays.[20]

The debate around gender remained largely ossified through the mid-twentieth century, with a few remarkable exceptions writing in radical journals like the *Kaumudi*, which were critical of the institutionalized Left, like K. Saraswati Amma (Devika 2003). The

[19]See, Editorial, 'Women's Social Mission' ('Streekalude Samoohyadautyam'), *Nazrani Deepika*, 2 August, 20 September, 1959.

[20]In the elections to the State legislature in 1960, for instance, there were four communist, three independent supported by communists and seven Congress candidates, 14 in all. *Nazrani Deepika* 10 January 1960.

silence was broken only in the late 1980s with the emergence of feminist groups. In the 1990s, these grew into full-fledged feminist politics, and with the fresh visibility gained with the coming of satellite television (which multiplied the sites of enunciation of gender issues), they challenged the sexism of the political organization, including the Left. The feminist movement in Kerala was battling with the state and political parties over cases of sexual harassment, precisely when an effort to gender governance, supposedly informed by global feminist perspectives on development was being prescribed and inserted in democratic decentralization (Devika and Kodoth 2001)! The formation of the Kerala State Women's Commission, intended as a step towards institutionalizing gender justice in the state, was ineffective. Predictably, the risk of the divisiveness within and between political parties getting reflected within the Women's Commission soon became a reality, and so did the deep resentment of powerful sections of the society (Erwer 2003: 169–74). Quotas for women in local governments brought a number of women into the political arena. Many of them developed the necessary skills. However, available studies point out that this has not begun to have a visible impact on politics or endow gender politics with a greater significance (Devika 2005).

DEVELOPMENT

Many of the first-generation feminists who sought to represent the interests of women in the 1930s and 1940s, shifted to development activism from the 1950s onwards. Many of them adopted the pattern of Gandhian social work.[21] What is worth noting is the extent to which development in the immediate post-independence period in India appeared like an eminently apolitical, or 'social' and inclusive activity. In the Community Development Project (CDP) of the 1950s women were addressed primarily as caregivers for the family, and encouraged to generate a home-based income. Up to the Fifth Plan, attention was paid largely to women's practical needs. Despite all efforts the Fourth Plan noted that most of the 2000 Mahila Samajams that existed in the state were dormant (Eapen 2000: 5–6). In fact, it

[21] Examples are many: Parvati Ayyapan; Konniyoor Meenakshi Amma; Ambady Kartyayani Amma; Akkamma Cheriyan; Mukkappuzha Kartyayani Amma and others.

was noted that even a project like the Indo-Norwegian Project which aimed at modernizing fishing and fish processing, and focused on the fishing community of south Kerala did not take into account women, though they were very clearly working and earning, presumably because they did not go out fishing (Gulati 1984). It has been pointed out that this did affect women negatively in the long run even if the project as a whole brought them some short-run gains (Dietrich and Nayak 2002). Mridul Eapen notes that it was from the Fifth Plan onwards that women began to be recognized as active participants in development (Eapen 2000:7). She notes however, that the results have been not optimal, for instance, in the Integrated Rural Development Programme (Eapen 2000:12). Other programmes of the 1970s also focussed on the practical gender needs of women. Eapen also remarks that despite efforts to improve women's employment and income generation capacities, '... with the implementation of the large ICDS project, there appears to be a re-emphasis on welfare measures for women since the Seventh Plan.' (Eapen 2000:12).

The Women Component Plan (WCP) of the Ninth Plan well-known as Kerala's innovation adopted in People's Planning which aimed at decentralizing governance and facilitating the entry of large numbers of women into local bodies, marking another watershed. Local bodies were expected to set apart 10 per cent as grant-in-aid for the WCP, for projects that directly benefited women. In the Gram Sabhas, gender was made a mandatory subject group; a chapter on women and development became compulsory in the panchayat development report. A gender impact statement for every project proposal and a separate task force to prepare projects specifically meant for women were also made mandatory. However, in the first year, there were serious failings. There were efforts to improve in the second year with the 10 per cent allocation to the WCP being ensured and a special gender-training programme instituted for women members (Mukherjee and Seema 2000).

Most of the available reports on gender in the experiment in decentralization and mainstreaming gender in governance and planning agree that the substantial reservation for women was definitely a major step towards inducting women as participants in local governance. They also point out that while those projects that were aimed at satisfying women's practical needs were generally endorsed, those that addressed their strategic interests were either ignored or opposed with, of course, some important exceptions

(Muralidharan 2003:3). Interestingly, projects that linked practical needs with strategic interests when the effort was to fulfil women's practical gender needs through means that essentially challenged entrenched forms of gender power, seemed to have provoked the greatest opposition (Vijayan and Sandhya 2004: 39). Projects that seemed to address women's livelihood without threatening the existent structures of gender dominance too explicitly, were not the target of opposition, though many of them died down, often due to the lack of managerial and entrepreneurial skills (Mukherjee and Seema 2000: 22, 47; Vijayan and Sandhya 2004: 39–42).

Recently, however, the state's innovative poverty eradication mission, the Kudumbashree, described as a 'woman-oriented poverty eradication mission', has attracted much attention. It has followed a multi-pronged strategy, which includes the convergence of various government programmes and resources at the level of community-based organizations, and development of women's micro-enterprises and thrift and credit societies. Women are reckoned to be the major agents of change not just because they assure better repayment rates but also because they are identified as being more vulnerable and implicitly responsible for the well-being of the family. 'Women's empowerment' is defined more or less, as increasing their capacity to improve the well-being of their families. It is assumed that the mutual synergies between better well-being, community improvement and participation in groups will lead on to the 'virtuous spiral' of women's empowerment. Women's participation in self-help groups is seen as a way to increase this empowerment.

Kudumbashree has elicited unprecedented response from below poverty level (BPL) women. Most importantly, several researchers have by now, noted that Kudumbashree women do display self-confidence and a sense of agency, despite serious lacunae in the scheme and poor incomes (Eapen and Thomas 2005: 61). It may be worth noting that besides the opportunities for saving and credit, and its linking to the panchayats, the most innovative part of Kudumbashree is its displacement of the image of the unpaid domestic woman from the domestic ideal and the installation of the image of the income-earning mother in its place. Given the fact that processes of individuation have been unleashed among the poorest women in Kerala partly due to their access to school education, and partly because the traditional caste society has been diminished to a very great extent this provides more space for their self-assertion. Especially important here is the fact that Kudumbashree mounts no direct challenge to prevailing gender hierarchies, and hence provides an opportunity for individual self-assertion within the terms of patriarchal institutions (Thampi and Devika 2005). The agency opened up by Kudumbashree thus falls squarely within the 'bargaining with patriarchy' framework, in which women seek a trade-off between consent to bourgeois patriarchy and her sharing of the structural capacities of the better-off, 'respectable' class as a (new) member (Sangari 2001: 282–91). This is particularly relevant for Kerala where social mobility aspirations are high and consumerist aspirations abound among all sections of the people, and not just the propertied middle class (Osella and Osella 2000). This is confirmed by recent work on gender norms and marriage strategies among Malayalee migrant women workers who have much larger incomes and bargaining power within their families (Gallo 2005).

Entrenched notions of women's economic roles are difficult to abandon. The transfer of the woman's share of property as dowry in the event of marriage has had serious consequences for women's property rights in Kerala (Kodoth, forthcoming). Despite this, the Mangalaya Scheme, an insurance plan for the destitute proposed in the 2004–5 Kerala State Budget, seems to endorse the transfer of resources meant for women at the time of their marriage: 'Under the proposed insurance scheme, Government will pay the monthly premium for a maximum period of eight years for every girl child from every destitute family above the age of fourteen. The amount so accrued, subject to a minimum of Rs10,000 will be given at the time of her marriage.'[22]

The above review reveals the extent to which far-reaching social change in the twentieth century Malayalee society that enabled effective empowerment of a wide section of the population through the extension of popular consciousness of basic rights, was also strongly mediated by a form of modern patriarchy. Thus while this democratization (Tharakan 1998) led to the achievement of high levels in many social development indicators, it gave women's status here an ambiguous twist. Therefore even as the minimal conditions for women's individuation were shaped neither education nor employment worked to strengthen these significantly, even though the physical quality of women's lives certainly improved.

[22]The Finance Minister's Budget Speech 2004–5, from http://kerala.gov.in/budget2004-2005/speech_eng.htm#_Toc62590022

II

A historical sociology of the Malayalee family that explores the gap between familial ideologies and present-day institutions is absent. Yet a few observations may be hazarded from the writings of the finest women authors in Malayalam, K. Saraswati Amma, and N. Lalitambika Antarjanam, who wrote in mid- and late twentieth-century, and observed the changing institutions of marriage and family. Early twentieth-century Malayalee community reformisms valorized the liberal notion of the domestic as a realm devoid of power and politics, characterized by sexual complementarity, not competition. This made the patriarchal power in the home invisible. Indeed, as Saraswati Amma observed, pre-modern patriarchal power could coexist in this domain with modern form—and this affected mainly the modern educated individuated woman (Devika 2003). However, Lalitambika Antarjanam reflected on the tensions generated by women's successful internalization of domestic ideology. Antarjanam acknowledged that the domestic role did involve the exercise of power, and that the homemaker was no passive domestic drudge. What she pointed to however, were the stresses and strains the woman had to bear to fulfill this role successfully (Devika 2001). This critique is distinct from the valorization of the enormously burdensome domestic role by other first generation feminists (Devika 2005a). Indeed, it rings relevant in the early twenty-first century Malayalee society, with the ideal of 'enlightened domesticity' gaining greater ground through the media (Osella and Osella 2000). The nature of domestic responsibility however has changed, becoming both heavier and more complex. Childcare has become 'child crafting' (Folbre 1998:134) with eyes increasingly fixed on the global job market. Making consumption decisions is taxing in the upswing of consumerism; mediating family ties more burdensome, with heightened migration. This multiplies familial tensions. It is then, hardly surprising that marital and family problems seem to figure high in the histories of suicides and attempted suicides by women in Kerala, as some studies show, the expectations are so high that stress levels may be pushed up enormously (Jayashree 2005).

The assumption that the ideal domestic woman will *automatically* gain authority within the household, however, needs to be questioned. This is not to deny the existence of 'domestic agency', which often gives some women considerable control over family members and family affairs, despite complete dependence on males in financial and public matters. However, such agency is not always forthcoming and does vary considerably across class and caste, available mostly to upper caste, upper class, and educated women. Besides, looking at the reported levels of domestic violence (Kodoth and Eapen 2005), there seems no guarantee that the woman who conforms will realize domestic agency; however, the woman who does not, pays a considerable price. Thus attempting to conform or making the show of conforming, seems to be as much a means of warding off negative consequences, as one to reaping positive gains. Moreover, there seems to be a 'bargain with patriarchy' in domestic agency, which makes it compliant to governmental measures but inimical to feminist politicization. Indeed, there is reason to think that for the majority of women in Kerala, active domestic agency remains either an unfulfilled promise or holds immense emotional burdens.

Gender constrains men too It draws him to the householder's interests eclipsing that of the citizen's (Devika 2002). The nature of truly 'manly' vocations and training has been debated in Kerala since early twentieth century (Devika 1998: 91–2). However, professional employment is still clearly the mark of masculine achievement. Recent research shows that men trained and employed as professionals are the highest-priced in the Malayalee marriage market (Osella and Osella 2000; Kodoth, forthcoming, 2006). Such training is ever more expensive and its pursuit, all the more stressful.

Yet women are definitely more constrained by gender. The ready conflation of the 'private' with the 'domestic' in Kerala constrains women more than men; for instance, young single women seeking private single accommodation is often treated as the surest sign of sexual profligacy.[23] Women have comparatively less mobility across social spaces—men have unrestrained access to the public, stronger 'homosocial' networks and spaces. (Osella and Osella 2004) Women are also disadvantaged by strong social compulsions to address domestic issues as moral or social pathological issues to be resolved through psychological and spiritual therapy rather than political ones. Thus feminist intervention in domestic turmoil is dubbed 'excessive', while those of familial, spiritual and 'moral' authorities and the 'experts' are welcomed. While equally subject to such pressures, men

[23]In April 2004, a controversy over the harassment of a young single working woman and short story writer, Sreebala K. Menon, sparked off a public discussion in which many single women spoke of such harassment. See 'Woman Complains against Residents' Association Office Bearers', *The Hindu*, 29 April 2004.

with greater access to independent incomes and homosocial networks may be much less vulnerable than those men who lack such access. Yet another way in which women are more constrained than men is related to soaring dowry rates. Marriage has become *the* major source of stress for young women and their families, given the high value of the marital tie for women.

Finally, the pervasiveness of gender in Kerala is also evident in emergent modes of self-assertion, which have little direct connection to either politics or development. An example is the neo-Hindu mode of 'empowering' women, well illustrated by the ordination of priestesses by Kerala's highly influential godwoman, Mata Amritanandamayi. In such 'empowerment', women are inserted, with the broader terms remaining unchanged, into institutions of faith. All restrictions applied traditionally to menstruating women, also apply to these priestesses. Men manage the public face of the organization while women carry out routine ritual worship. Thus this 'gain' does not seem unsettling of gender norms(Warrier 2005). Another instance of retaining gender inequality is that of the new identities accessed through consumption, which also seem strongly gendered. Young women are saddled with negotiating between local patriarchal values and the possibilities of consumption to a much higher degree (Lukose 2005: 931).

Thus, both 'productivist masculinity' and 'domestic femininity' bring in their wake different if interrelated, stress for both men and women. Gender regulates even those who seek to access modes of self-assertion not defined in any significant sense by society or development. Women however, are more vulnerable to gender oppression than men—though neither domesticity nor distance from the public renders them entirely passive. Secondly, Kerala's 'gender paradox' hardly appears paradoxical if one is prepared to shed the assumption that better social development indicators will lead to women's emancipation. Rather, one must pay attention to the broader contexts of social reform and political-governmental intervention, both of which fostered new forms of patriarchy.

To conclude, one cannot help but comment on the astonishing similarities between the sources of patriarchy critiqued by first- and second-generation feminists in Kerala. For instance, through the century, women writing in popular magazines have protested against the steady expansion of dowry. From the mid-century to the present, they have spoken against the marginalization of gender issues within the society, and the instrumentalist use of women in political mobilization (Devika

2006b). These generations differed immensely in the anti-patriarchal suggestions they put forward. However, both the generations complain with equal vehemence that emergent institutions such as the modern field of politics and the family are thoroughly saturated with misogyny. This, we feel, is significant with regard to the nature, solidity, and strength of modern patriarchy in Kerala.

REFERENCES

Amma, T.D., 1924–5, 'The Goal of Female Education (Streevidyabhyasathinte Uddesham)' in *Lakshmi Bhayi*, 20 (1), pp. 36–8.

Amma, Kalyani B., 1968, 'Ormayil Ninnu', B. Gomathy Amma (ed.), *Sahitya Pravartaka Sahakarana Sangham*, Kottayam: SPSS.

Amma, K.M., 2005 [1925], 'Nair Women and the Home (*Nair Streekalum Grhavum*)', J. Devika, (ed. and trans.), *Her-Self: Early Writings on Gender by Malayalee Women*, Kolkata: Stree, pp. 88–92.

Awaya, T., 1996, 'Women in the Nambutiri "Caste" Movement', T. Mizushima and H. Yanagisawa (eds.), *History and Society in South India*, Tokyo: Tokyo University of Foreign Studies, pp. 47–57.

Basheer, K.P.M., 2004, 'The Gulf Wife Syndrome', Mohan Rao (ed.), *The Unheard Scream: Reproductive Health and Women's Lives*, New Delhi: Zubaan and Panos, pp. 148–67.

Begum, M.R., 2001, 'Prevalence of Malnutrition among Adolescent Girls in a Rural Area: A Case Study in Kalliyoor Panchayat, Thiruvananthapuram', discussion Paper 35, KRP, Thiruvananthapuram: Centre For Development Studies.

Bhaskarunny, P., 1988, *Pattonpatam Nootandile Keralam*, Thrissur: Kerala Sahitya Akademi.

Bhattatiripad, V.T., 1988, *Karmavipakam*, Changanasery: Best Books.

Census of India, 1931.

Chandy, A., 2005 [1929], 'On Women's Liberation (*Streeswatantryate Patti*)' J. Devika, (ed. and trans.), *Her-Self: Early Writings on Gender by Malayalee Women*, Kolkata: Stree, pp. 113–29.

Chacko, I.C., 2005 [1927], 'Our Women (*Nammude Streekal*)', J. Devika, (ed. and trans.), *Her-Self: Early Writings on Gender by Malayalee Women*, Kolkata: Stree, pp. 96–105.

Chasin, B.H., 1990, 'Land Reform and Women's Work in a Kerala Village', working paper 207, Women in International Development, Michigan: Michigan State University.

Chatterjee, P., 1989, 'The Nationalist Resolution of the Women's Question', K. Sangari and S. Vaid (eds.), *Recasting Women: Essays in Colonial History*, New Delhi: Kali for Women, pp. 233–48.

Collins, 1990 [1877], *Ghatakavadham* (*The Slayer Slain*), Kottayam: D.C. Books.

Devayani, K., 1995, 'Alappuzhayile Stree Munnettangal', Paper presented at the seminar, 'Women in Kerala: Past and Present', 11–12 February, Thiruvananthapuram.

Devi, R., 2004, *From the Dusk of Life: The Autobiography of Ratnamayi Devi*, New Delhi: Konark Publishers.

Devi, L., 2002, 'Education, Employment and Job Preferences of Women in Kerala: A Micro Level Study', discussion Paper 42, KRP, Thiruvananthapuram: Centre For Development Studies.

Devika, J., 1998, 'En-Gendering Individuals: A Study of Gender and Individualisation in Reform-language in Modern Keralam', Ph.D. thesis, Kottayam: Mahatma Gandhi University.

____ 2001, 'Unnameable Discontents: Individualism and Gender in the Writings of Lalitambika Antarjanam', Paper presented at seminar 'Rethinking Modernity', 16–18 November, Department of Philosophy, Kalady: Shree Sankara University of Sanskrit.

____ 2002, 'Domesticating Malayalees: Family Planning, The Nation and Home-centred Anxieties', working Paper 340, Thiruvananthapuram: Centre for Development Studies.

____ 2003, 'Beyond "Kulina" and "Kulata": The Critique of Gender Differences in the writings of K. Saraswati Amma', *Indian Journal of Gender Studies*, 10(2), pp. 201–28.

____ 2005, 'Modernity with Democracy? Gender and Governance in the People's Planning Campaign, Keralam', working Paper 368, Thiruvananthapuram: Centre for Development Studies.

____ 2005a, *Her-Self: Early Writings on Gender by Malayalee Women 1898–1938*, Kolkata: Stree.

____ 2005b, 'The Malayali Sexual Revolution: Sex, Liberation and Family Planning in Kerala', *Contributions to Indian Sociology*, 39 (3), pp. 343–76.

____ 2006, 'Negotiating Women's Space: Public Debates on Gender in Early Modern Kerala, India', *Inter-Asia Cultural Studies* 7 (1), pp. 43–61.

____ 2006a, 'The Housewife, the Sex-Worker, and the Re-former: Life-Writing and the Resistance to Modern Patriarchy in Kerala', *Economic and Political Weekly*, Vol. 41, No. 17, pp. 1675–83.

____ (ed.) 2006b, *Aanarashunaattile Kazchakal: Kerala Streepakshagaveshanathil (Sights from Male-dom: Kerala in Feminist Research)*, Thiruvananthapuram: Women's Imprint.

____ 2007, *En-gendering Individuals: The Language of Re-forming in Early Twentieth Century Keralam*, New Delhi: Orient Longman.

Devika, J. and Kodoth, P., 2001, 'Sexual Violence and the Predicament of Feminist Politics in Kerala', *Economic and Political Weekly*, Vol. 36, No. 33, pp. 3170–7.

Dietrich, G. and Nayak, N., 2002, 'Transition or Transformation? A Study of the Mobilisation, Organisation and Emergence of Consciousness among the Fishworkers of Kerala, India', Madurai: Tamilnadu Theological Seminary.

Eapen, M., 1992, 'Fertility and Female Labour Force Participation in Kerala', *Economic and Political Weekly*, Vol. 27, No. 21, pp. 2179–88.

____ 2000, 'Gender and Governance: Reviewing Kerala's Five Year Plans', Paper presented at Workshop 'Gender and Governance', 5–6 August, Bangalore.

Eapen, M. and Thomas, S., 2005, 'Gender Analysis of select Gram (Village) Panchayat Plan Budgets in Trivandrum District, Kerala', discussion Paper 11, New Delhi: HDRC and UNDP.

Erwer, M., 2003, 'Challenging the Gender Paradox-Women's Collective Agency in the Transformation of Kerala Politics', Ph.D. Thesis, Department of Peace and Development Research, Göteborg: Göteborg University.

Folbre, N., 1998, 'Patriarchy and Fertility Decisions', P. Demeny and G.M. Nicolls (eds.), *The Earthscan Reader in Population and Development*, London: Earthscan, pp. 121–42.

Forbes, G., 2000, *Women in Modern India, The New Cambridge History of India IV.2*, Cambridge: Cambridge University Press.

Gallo, E., 2005, 'Unorthodox Sisters: Gender Relations and Generational Changes in Transnational Malayali Marriages', Paper presented at KCHR Colloquium, 5 February, Thiruvananthapuram.

George, S.M., 1999, 'Gendered Ideologies and Strategies: The Negotiation of the Household Division of Labour among Middle-Class South Asian American Families', working Paper 8, Centre for Working Families, Berkeley: University of California.

Gopalakrishnan, K.G., 1987, *Vimochanasamaram—Oru Padhanam*, Attingal: Nakshatram Books.

Gopalakrishnan, P.K., 1994, *Keralattinte Samskarikacharitram*, Thiruvananthapuram: State Institute of Languages.

Gulati, L., 1983, 'Impact of the Development Process on the Indian Family', working Paper 174, Thiruvananthapuram: Centre for Development Studies.

____, 1984, 'Fisherwomen on the Kerala Coast: Demographic and Socio-Economic Impact of a Fisheries Development Project', Geneva: International Labour Organization.

Haggis, J., 2000, 'Ironies of Emancipation: Changing Configurations of Women's Work in the "Mission of Sisterhood" to Indian Women', *Feminist Review*, 65 (1), pp. 108–26.

Isaac, T.M., Franke, R.W. and Raghavan, P., 1998, *Democracy at Work: An Indian Industrial Cooperative The Story of Dinesh Beedi*, Ithaca: Cornell University Press.

Jayashree, A.K., 2005, 'Gender Issues in Suicide: A Study among Suicide Attempters Admitted to the Thiruvananthapuram General Hospital during 1994–5', http://www.thrani.org/pdf/suigen.pdf.

Jefferey, R., 2003, *Politics, Women and Well-Being—How Kerala became a Model*, New Delhi: Oxford University Press.

Jong, M.A. De, 2004, 'Moral Dress for Modern Women: Female Muslim

Students in Kerala—Interpreting the Veil', M.A. Thesis, Amsterdam: University of Amsterdam.

Kannan, K.P., 2005, 'Turnaround in Growth: Role of Social Development, Remittances and Reform', *Economic and Political Weekly*, Vol. 40, No. 6, pp. 548–54.

Kodoth, P., 2001, 'Sexuality, Sambandham and Marriage in Late Nineteenth Century Malabar', *Modern Asian Studies*, 35 (2), pp. 349–84.

____ 2006, '*Varante Vila Uyarunnu: Lingadhikaravum Vivahalochanayum Keralattil* (The Rising Price of Men: Gender in Marriage Match-making in Kerala)', J. Devika, (ed.), *Aanarashunattile Kazhcchakal: Keralam Streepakshagaveshanattil* (Sights in Male-dom: Kerala in Feminist Research), Thiruvananthapuram: Women's Imprint.

Kodoth, P. and Eapen, M., 2005, 'Looking Beyond Gender Parities: Gender Inequities of Some Dimensions of Well-Being in Kerala', *Economic and Political Weekly*, Vol. 40, No. 30, pp. 3278–86.

Krishnan, N. R.; 1958, *Smarana Vol. II*, Chertala.

Kumar, R., 1994, 'Development and Women's Work in Kerala: Interactions and Paradoxes', *Economic and Political Weekly*, Vol. 29, Nos. 51–2, pp. 3249–54.

Lindberg, A., 2001, 'Experience and Identity: A Historical Account of Class, Caste, Gender among the Cashew Workers of Kerala, 1930–2000', Ph.D. Thesis, Department of History, Lund: Lund University.

Lukose, R., 2005, 'Consuming Globalization: Youth and Gender in Kerala, India', *Journal of Social History*, 38(4), pp. 915–35.

Mateer, S., 1991 [1883], *Native Life in Travancore*, New Delhi: Asia Educational Services.

Menon, D.M., 1994, *Caste, Nationalism and Communism in South India: Malabar, 1900–1948*, Cambridge: Cambridge University Press.

Menon, L., 2003, 'Health of the Kerala Ms. on the Slide', *The Hindu (Kochi Edition) Metro Plus*, 25 August.

Menon, O.C., 1989 [1889], *Indulekha*, Kottayam: D.C. Books.

Menon, P.K.K., 1972, 'History of the Freedom Movement in Kerala', Vol. 2, Thiruvananthapuram: Kerala State Gazetteers Department.

Misra, U.S. and Ramanathan, M., 2001, 'Delivery Complications and Determinants of Caesarean Section Rates in India—An Analysis of National Family Health Surveys', working Paper 314, Thiruvananthapuram: Centre for Development Studies.

Mukherjee, V.N. and Seema, T.N., 2000, 'Gender, Governance and Decentralized Planning: The Experience and People's Campaign in Kerala', paper presented at International Conference on Democratic Decentralization, 20–23 May, Thiruvananthapuram.

Muralidharan, S., 2003, 'Gender and Decentralization: Opportunities and Challenges', *Kerala Calling*, October, pp. 21–4.

Nair, C.C., 1985 [1892], *Meenakshi*, Thrissur: Kerala Sahitya Akademi.

Nair, K.G. and Pushpa, B., 1992, *Charitrattinte Aedukal (988–1022)*, Thiruvananthapuram: Irayimman Thampi Smaraka Padhanakendram.

Nair, N.B., 1947, *K. Chinnamma: Jeevacharitram*, Thiruvananthapuram: Sri Vilas Press.

Nambutiripad, E.M.S., 1945, *Nambutiriye Manushyanakkan*, Kozhikode: Deshabhimani Publications.

Niuewenhuys, O., 1999, *Children's Lifeworlds: Gender, Welfare and Labour in the Developing World*, New Delhi: Social Science Press.

O' Hanlon, R., 2000, *A Comparison between Women and Men: Tarabai Shinde and the Critique of Gender Relations in Colonial India*, New Delhi: Oxford University Press.

Osella, F. and Osella, C., 2000, *Social Mobility in Kerala: Modernity and Identity in Conflict*, London: Pluto Press.

____ 2004, 'Young Malayali Men and their Movie Heroes', R. Chopra, F. Osella and C. Osella (eds.), *South Asian Masculinities: Context of Change, Sites of Continuity*, New Delhi: Women Unlimited, pp. 224–61.

Panikar, P.G.K. and Soman, C.R., 1984, 'Health Status of Kerala—The Paradox of Economic Backwardness and Health Development', Thiruvananthapuram: Centre for Development Studies.

Pillai, K.A.G., 1977, *Mannattinte Sampoorna Kritikal*, Kottayam: Vidyarthimitram.

Pushpangadhan, K. and Murugan, G., 2000, 'Gender Bias in a Marginalised Community: A Study of Fisherfolk in Coastal Kerala', working Paper 302, Thiruvananthapuram: Centre for Development Studies.

Riley, D., 1995, *'Am I that Name'—Feminism and the Category of 'Women' in History*, Minneapolis: University of Minnesota Press.

Rajan, S.I., Sudha, S. and Mohanachandran, P., 2000, 'Fertility Decline and Worsening Gender Bias in India: Is Kerala No Longer an Exception?', *Development and Change*, 31, 5, pp. 1085–92.

Rammohan, K.T., 1996, 'Material Processes and Developmentalism: Understanding Economic Change in Tiruvitamkoor 1800–1945', Ph.D. Thesis, Thiruvananthapuram: Centre for Development Studies.

Report of the Administration of Tiruvitamkoor (1868–69).

____ (1869–70).

Report of the Tiruvitamkoor Educational Reforms Committee 1933.

Sangari, K., 2001, *Politics of the Possible: Essays on Gender, History, Narratives, Colonial English*, New Delhi: Tulika.

Sardamony, K., 1999, *Matriliny Transformed: Family, Law and Ideology in Twentieth Century Tiruvitamkoor*, London and New Delhi: Sage Publications and Altamira Press.

Sarkar, T., 1996, 'Colonial Lawmaking and Lives/Deaths of Indian Women: Different Readings of Law and Community', in R. Kapur (ed.), *Feminist Terrains in Legal Domains: Interdisciplinary Essays on Women and Law in India*, New Delhi: Kali for Women, pp. 210–42.

Soman, C.R., 2004, 'The Time Bomb that Ticks ... The Future of Kerala's Health', *Kerala Calling*, January, pp. 22–4.

Thampi, B.V. and Devika, J., 2005, 'Changing Regimes of Empowerment and Inclusion in the Public: Women and the *Kudumbashree* in Contemporary

Kerala', paper presented at conference 'A Decade of Decentralisation in Kerala: Issues, Options and Lessons', 7–9 October, Thiruvananthapuram.

Tharakan, M., 1998, 'Socio-Religious Reform Movements, the Process of Democratization and Human Development: The Case of Kerala, South West India', L. Rudebeck and O. Tornquist (eds.), *Democratization in the Third World: Concrete Cases in Comparative and Theoretical Perspectives,* London: Macmillan, pp. 69–89.

Uyl, M. den, 1995, *Invisible Barriers: Gender, Caste and Kinship in a Southern Indian Village,* Utrecht: International Books.

Velayudhan, M., 1994, 'Changing Roles and Women's Narratives', *Social Scientist,* 22: 1–2, (248–9), pp. 64–79.

____ 1999, 'Reform, Law and Gendered Identity', M. A. Oommen (ed.), *Rethinking Development: Kerala's Experiences-Vol I,* New Delhi: Institute of Social Research and Concept Publishers, pp. 60–72.

____ 1999a. 'The Growth of Political Consciousness among Women in Modern Kerala', P. J. Cheriyan (ed.), *Perspectives on Kerala History, Kerala State Gazetteer Vol. 2, Part I,* Thiruvananthapuram: Government of Kerala.

Vijayan, A. and Sandhya, J., 2004, 'Gender and Decentralized Planning, Kerala, India', SAKHI Thiruvananthapuram: Women's Resource Centre.

Warrier, M., 2005, *Hindu Selves in a Modern World: Guru Faith in the Mata Amritanandamayi Mission,* London: Routledge Curzon.

Zachariah, K.C., Mathew, E.T. and Rajan, S.I., 2003, *Dynamics of Migration in Kerala: Dimensions, Differentials and Consequences,* Hyderabad: Orient Longman.

SECTION 2

Living as a Woman
Some Case Studies

This section contains edited versions of a few selected narratives on the life histories of women as they were related to researchers.[1] The narratives suggest that the average woman in Kerala is perhaps not very different from the average woman elsewhere in the country. Marriage is central to her life; her relationship with her husband defines her destiny. Entrenched belief in traditional gender norms runs as an unstated yet pervasive theme throughout the narratives. Most stories also seem to bear a tinge of understated resignation and sadness about them, as if the women have been mute witnesses to the course their lives have taken, accepting whatever has come their way.

Violence does not figure much in these narratives, except in a couple of cases, which specifically refer to having seriously alcoholic males in the households. Women may subscribe to norms of male dominated households, or may have a few fall back options. They may internalize abuse, and desist from talking about it. Yet (although reliable comparative figures are not available) it is believed that the

[1]These narratives are edited versions of seven of the nineteen case studies carried out during the first phase of the Gender Network Project. Dr T.K. Anandy with assistance from Sandhya Chandrasekharan, Geeta and Bindu carried out the studies in north and central Kerala while the work in Trivandrum was carried out by Ms. Deepa Shankar of the Department of Psychology, University of Kerala, with the help of N. Meera. All the case studies appear in the Appendix to the report prepared by Eapen and Kodoth (2001) in the first phase of Gender Network research. Names of the respondents have been changed to ensure anonymity.

incidence of alcoholism is rather high in Kerala. Alcoholism among men is one of the major proximate factors behind the high incidence of discord and violence within the home. As discussed in the introductory chapter, a complex juxtaposition of factors may have been responsible for this situation in the state. But again, one would expect this to be understated in the narratives.

In an interesting case study included here, where the woman grows up in an atmosphere steeped in Left ideology and eventually marries one of her fellow comrades, she finds to her dismay, that the doctrine of class exploitation has no counterpart in matters of gender. This does not surprise one. In spite of its long and pervasive presence in the political scenario of the state, the Left movement has had little to offer by way of genuine gender equity.

It is clear from all the narratives that, by and large, these women did not suffer any significant gender discrimination during their growing up years, which is not something that one can vouch for in some other parts of the country. For the women in these stories, the travails of belonging to the 'second sex' started manifesting themselves after they reached puberty, and then, if anything, got worse only after marriage. Recent evidence on increased female foeticide in the state suggests that things may have been changing for the worse for young girls in Kerala.

These case studies offer an intimate glimpse into the everyday lives of a few women from varied backgrounds. It is hoped that they will complement the analytical content of the text and provide a human face to the enigmatic woman of Kerala.

Editor

Sakina

My father died twenty-seven years ago when I was only a child. My mother is seventy years old now. I am one of seven children. One of my elder brothers, an elder sister and my younger brother are no more. I am married and have two children. My husband used to sell fish. Presently he is in a mental hospital. I have a son and a daughter. We are fourth 'Veda' Muslims.

I was born in Trivandrum. My father was a scrap dealer. He was away a lot, because he went to auctions. My elder brother brought all of us up. Mother did not work. I do not remember when my father died. I was told that he (father) was in the hospital when I asked for him. My mother was married at the age of nine and at sixteen, she delivered my elder brother. I do not know what the relationship between my parents was like.

My brother looked after us. He was twenty-one years old when father died. I studied up to the fifth standard. After my father died I had to ask my brother for books and uniforms. He told me that it was difficult to provide books and asked me to stop studying. Moreover, I failed in the fifth standard. My sisters are not educated either. My elder brother studied up to class three. It was only because I insisted that he sent me to school.

I used to do work in the household when I was small. My sister-in-law forced me to do housework, and if I made a mistake she would get angry and scold me. I was sad about that and would cry a lot.

I used to ask my mother why she did not remarry. A stepfather might have taken on my responsibility and I need not have suffered like this. My brother got married when I was seven years old. My mother is afraid of my brother. Her word does not count in front of him or his wife.

I attained puberty when I was fifteen years old. They did not allow me to go out after that. I was not taken anywhere and was told that only after marriage would I be allowed to go out again. Similar restrictions were followed for my older sisters also. We have a celebration for coming of age. In the house, they were happy and my relatives gave me money with which the function for seven days was performed. There are also restrictions on talking to men. I was allowed to speak to my uncle's son and other relatives, but I could not go out without my brother's permission. I was afraid of him. During their menses, women were not allowed to go out at all. But now things are different and everyone is allowed to go out. When my mother was young, they were not even allowed to change their dress or take a bath for seven days during the menstrual cycle. When I was young, on the seventh day, we were told to clean the places where we moved around in the house. We had to sprinkle water and chant hymns to make the place pure. Some people still follow these traditions. But if we tell my brother's daughters to follow the same customs and practice, will they obey us?

Only after my marriage did I see the outside world. I had not gone out even once after I attained menarche except to mosques and hospitals. I had never been for movies or any other happy functions. But now my brothers' daughters go with my sister's husband. This is a new age. My times were different.

During my childhood, I do not remember having any significant illnesses but now I'm ill all the time. We (husband and I) decided to have only two children because I'm not healthy. I have had a hysterectomy.

As a child, I was afraid of my brother and never thought of disobeying him. He would punish and beat us. Once when I was home, I had referred to someone without the correct term of respect and my brother punished me severely. When I was a child, everybody was served with similar kind of food by my mother. But my sister-in-law would be partial in serving food to my brother (her husband). Generally men are served first.

I got married when I was about twenty-seven years old; I do not remember exactly whether it was twenty-five, twenty-six or twenty-seven, but it was around that age. I know because it was a late marriage.

Since I had lost my father in childhood, my brother was responsible for arranging my marriage. Whenever any proposal came, my brother used to say that he did not have the means to provide for a dowry. Several marriage proposals were rejected because of that and I became saddened by this rejection of proposals. There was no one to whom I could show my feelings, not even my mother.

The boys' families would ask for Rs 50,000 and ten sovereigns of gold but I was not given that much. I was given five sovereigns of gold and Rs 15,000 as cash—a total of Rs 30,000. My husband's job was selling fish. Both our families are of the same status.

My brother's daughters are married now. To get his two daughters married, my brother sold all the property at Thamalam for Rs 7,00,000 and now we live in a house rented for Rs 2,500 per month. The first daughter was given Rs 3,00,000 as dowry. She is a graduate and her husband supplies spices to shops at Ernakulam. He is a postgraduate and gets more than Rs 4,000 per month. My brother gave him 20 gold sovereigns, two and a half cents of land, a Rado watch worth Rs 10–17,000 and a ring. My brother's second daughter was also given Rs 2,50,000 as dowry. The balance amount was spent for my brother's son to go abroad. He was working in some vegetable shop abroad and was brought back as he had some mental illness on the fourth day itself. He was afraid to board a flight, scared that it would catch fire and finally he came back looking as if he were dead and was treated in the medical college hospital. Now he is all right.

My husband has four sisters and an elder brother. Four of them were unmarried at the time of our marriage and we were told that he had only two younger sisters. But after I went to their house I found he had four sisters. My father-in-law had a *beedi* shop. He must be over 60 years now. My mother-in-law's mother also stayed with us then. Only my husband's elder brother was married and was living separately with his wife and two children.

First when I was married, it was fine. Then in later years, some problems cropped up with my sister-in-law. They (husband's family) had four cents of land and four girls to be married. When the elder one got married, my husband gave her Rs 5,000 and a ring of mine. He pledged one of my chains for Rs 2,000. The second sister was also given Rs 5,000 with the money that my husband got from a chit fund, and two or three gold sovereigns. The third sister was given one and a half cents of land and two gold sovereigns and the fourth sister was given two cents of land and four gold sovereigns. No cash was given to the third and fourth sisters. Actually, the land was given by my father-in-law. But for the older two sisters, my husband gave the money.

The house was renovated with the money I brought as dowry and that house has been given to the fourth daughter. I wasn't told about that—my husband did it without even speaking to me about it. When I asked him he denied that the money was from my dowry. Now we don't have even a rented house. For the last one year we don't have even a single cent of land of our own. My in-laws rented a house after their daughters' marriages, and now they are living in a house they made on public land (Porumboke). We have been asked to vacate the rented house.

When we got married, my husband used to drink occasionally. Before we got married I didn't know that he drank, in fact, even my in-laws were unsure whether their son drank or not. One day before we were married, my uncle enquired after my husband's whereabouts and no one knew where he was. Later on my husband told me that he was actually in a toddy shop at that time.

I did not want this marriage. I objected from the very beginning. It was only after we got married that I realized that my husband was a fish-seller. When he came to see me before we got married I was not allowed to speak to him so I did not know what he was like. He came with seven or eight friends and no females. We saw each other, and I did not like him even then. My brother's wife said to everyone that there was no reason to get my consent and approval for the marriage because I was going to be married off to this very man no matter what I said. Eventually I said yes for this match. I think I said yes because I was afraid of my brother. I feel the sufferings I bore when I lived in my brother's house are the same as the sufferings I bear after my marriage. The only difference is that I am in a different place. My husband did not take me out anywhere after we got married. I did not have a single day in my life, which was happy for me. If there was some function or ceremony I was sent along with my mother in law.

I have a son and a daughter. My son is twelve years old and daughter is ten years old. Although I have got offers for work I do not go, because my husband does not want me to work and has told me not to go for these jobs. I was very eager to continue my studies and also find a job. I still regret not continuing my studies. If I had continued I might have had a job today.

At first, my husband used to drink only occasionally and it was not a problem. It increased after he became mentally ill, two and a half years ago. After my marriage I was ill. I had headaches, back pain, joint pain, and excessive bleeding. We did not have a happy sexual life. Maybe this was the reason he started drinking more and more. Somehow we had two children. When he came home drunk, I would get angry with him. In the last two or three years, his drinking has increased further. When he is drunk, he beats me up and accuses me of having an illicit relationship with my brother's son. My nephew is my own flesh and blood and my husband's accusations hurt a lot. Because of this my brother has told me to leave my husband.

My father-in-law also drinks but generally my in-laws are good to me. My husband is different from everyone else. He doesn't know what he is doing or what he is saying once he is drunk. He abuses others using filthy words and has even threatened to harm his parents. During the early days of our marriage he did not physically abuse me. Now he finds any excuse to beat me up. I think his drinking is related to his mental health. Initially when we got married we were able to talk freely about personal matters with each other. But now, once he drinks, he becomes unpredictable. He has even beaten the children.

At one point our life was settling down a little and had returned to some normalcy. My brother found a house for us to rent. It was not even one week after we shifted that he walked into the kitchen drunk, and caught me by my hair and beat me up. I didn't say anything or retaliate because it would have made things worse. Out of desperation I took him to the mosque and made him swear in front of God that he wouldn't beat our children or me. He did that and promised he would stop. It lasted twenty days and we were so happy for those days. And then for the last two years, it has been the same.

I found out from my mother-in-law that he was having an affair with a woman in the neighbourhood, who worked in a school as a cook. When I asked my husband he denied it strongly. Then he told me that even if it had happened it was my fault because I was incapable and couldn't take care of his needs.

Sometimes he makes things up. He thinks that everyone is talking about him. And for a long time he would say that someone was coming with a knife to kill him. One day, four of his friends brought him to me. They told me that they thought he had some kind of illness and asked me to take him to my home. That's when I took him to a doctor who referred him to a psychiatrist. While he was in hospital he would tell me that he was going to kill my brother, Shaji, my brother's son and me. When they gave him a drip in the hospital, he became scared that we were having him killed.

Recently, in front of a lot of people he told me that I could not satisfy him sexually and therefore he had to pay Rs 10–50 for women who could take care of him properly. That depressed me, especially because he said these things in front of outsiders. When he does something wrong to me, I never blame him in front of others, because he is my husband. I have to bear everything he does. I am powerless.

Now, I take care of him. But if he misbehaves anymore I will divorce him. I swear in the name of my daughter that I will leave him. If he drinks, beats or doubts me anymore after this I'll leave him.

I think living in a nuclear family is good. We had wished to have two children, the first a boy and the second a girl and we have got as we wished, and are satisfied. Since we have a daughter we should save some money for her marriage, but for that we have to live separately from the rest of the family. In a joint family, it is impossible to save any money. Not only that, if we are in a nuclear family set up, my husband will be more responsible and interested to make money. In a joint family we spend all the money for the family and give all the fish my husband gets, to them. Our children have grown up. How long shall we continue our life like this by sharing food with our relatives? I want them to get married and would like to buy some ornaments for my daughter.

Vasanthathukutty

My name is Vasanthathukutty. It is an old name. I do not know how old I am, but when somebody asks, I say I am sixty-five years old. I live in Chelurpadam, Malappuram district with my children. My natal house is in Ramanattukara. I have one elder sister and two brothers. Father ran his own business. My husband runs a provision store.

I have eight children. The first three are girls. Then, the fourth is a boy. The next one is again a girl, who lives with me because the school where she teaches is nearby. The last three boys live in Mysore running the business with their father. My eldest son works for the daily newspaper *Malayala Manorama*, and three of my daughters are teachers. My eldest son's wife is also a teacher. They were married only two months ago.

My natal house was a well known *tarawad*, and I had a very happy life there. We had helpers to wash clothes and look after the children. My father had two wives so we had two mothers to look after us. Though my father used to be very fond of us, especially me (I never used to eat or sleep without him), and took special care of my mother, he married another woman, that too, an Ezhava woman. After his second marriage he started living with his new wife. My mother, who was a very calm and quiet woman, told him one day that we were missing our father, so he better bring her home and we could all stay together. My father made his second wife a Muslim. And you won't believe it, my mother and her co-wife got along like sisters.

But later, after my marriage, I took my mother along with me and the second wife stayed with him.

I never saw my mother and father fighting with each other. Even after his second marriage, my father never lost interest in my mother or us. He used to wash my hair, tie it, oil it and keep me neat and clean. He also helped mother and gave her money regularly.

Our school was nearby, but on the way, there was a place where *harijans* (*cherumakkal*) were buried. Some people believed that there were evil spirits in that area. My parents, being superstitious, refused to send us to school and stopped our education. My teachers used to like me because I studied hard and did well in class..

I was married at the age of twelve, and attained puberty after my marriage. Normally, there is no 'seeing the girl' ceremony. The elders decide the *mehr* money and dowry and ornaments. We have no voice. *Puthukkam* is the ceremony when the boy and girl begin to live together as husband and wife. That is when the marriage is consummated. My husband was twenty two years old at the time of our marriage. My sister was married at the age of eleven and three years later, she had her *puthukkam*. After the *nikah*, the girl can stay in her own house. *Mehr* refers to the money given by the boy for the girl, and belongs to her by right if he dissolves the marriage. It is calculated according to the number of gold sovereigns given to the girl. I was given a gold chain and gold bangles, as well as Rs 75 as my dowry. My husband was given a golden ring. My *nikah* and *puthukkam* took place on the same day.

Like I said before, I attained puberty in my husband's house. My sister-in-law noticed it first. I did not know much about puberty at that time, other than what we had been taught in the *madrasa*. In my natal home we had never observed distance pollution or purity rituals. Now, for the first time, I wasn't allowed to enter the male area of the house. Usually there is a small ceremony and relatives give gifts of gold and dresses for the girl. My natal home was close by so my parents hosted a small feast for me and dressed me up in new clothes and jewellery.

In my husband's home we had a lot of different problems. When I came to his house, it was a joint family with two sisters-in-law, two brothers-in-law and my father-in-law and mother-in-law. *Bappa* (father) did not live at home but used to visit once in two or three years. They told me that *Bappa* and my husband were running the business jointly when I got married, but after I went to live in their house, it became clear that this was not so. They were splitting the business and doing completely separate things. That was the time when we had real financial problems. Sometimes we even had to sell cooking vessels or ornaments for food. Later when my sisters-in-law and brothers-in-law were married, our problems decreased.

In my natal home, we had a good life. But after I got married I never stayed there permanently. Though we are allowed to go home whenever we want to and spend time there, we are not supposed to get any financial help from our parents or brothers.

One of my sisters-in-law was divorced three times. For all three marriages, my husband had to go and bring her back home. Then we would start looking for a husband again, and within a year or two, she would divorce him. Every marriage created a heavy financial burden for my husband. None of the men gave back the dowry or ornaments and *mehr*. We lost a lot of money because of her marriages. There were never these kinds of problems in my family. No *talaq* (divorce) has taken place in my family.

My real problem was poverty. I had to work hard; pounding *nellu*, husking rice, preparing food. I had never done this much work in my own house. Thankfully, my husband was not particular; he had no preferences or demands at all.

My pregnancies and deliveries were never a happy event, because of our financial problems. I had my first child, a daughter, when I was eighteen years old, and then my second daughter was born, three years later. The other six children were all born at two-year intervals. We never considered family planning in those days. All my deliveries were performed by a nurse (*vayatatti*) at home. Except for the first delivery, I never had proper post-natal care. Perhaps because of that, I had severe bleeding some years back and had to undergo an operation for prolapsed uterus. Now I have no complications.

Though I had relatives all around me, I feel that I have really suffered. I had to ask my mother for everything. When the children were ill, I had no other option but to give them local medicine. I could not even afford to take them to the doctor.

I remember when my son was a year old he had dysentery and we had to take him to the Medical College. The doctors there had to admit him and I was so worried. Only Allah knows how much I suffered. My son was not even able to breathe properly. It took him a week to get all right, but by then, my three daughters had also fallen sick and were vomiting severely. I remember I only had one rupee with me, but I had to admit the children in hospital. Two were in the Medical College and two were in the Beach hospital. It was a very difficult time for me and what made it worse was that my husband was not there to help. It was always like that—he was never there when there was a crisis.

Joint families have their own advantages and disadvantages. You don't have to worry so much about the youngsters or even the elderly people in a joint family. You need not bother even if you get pregnant every year. There are always others at home who will help to take care of the young ones. A woman's, especially a young mother's anxieties are reduced in a joint family. A nuclear family is very different—you have to do everything yourself. You don't have anybody to help you. Moreover you feel very lonely.

But at the same time, joint families have their disadvantages. The women in the family come from different backgrounds, and problems start. I experienced the negative aspects of a joint family as well. Initially, I was on very good terms with my mother-in-law, but then my husband's aunt came to stay with us. This aunt told my mother-in-law that I did some *koodothram* (black magic) to her and my mother-in-law believed her. Everybody at home, including my husband was against me. I even thought of committing suicide but didn't, because of my children. Later, things returned to normal between my mother-in-law and me, but the incident had affected me and upset me too much for everything to be fine again. Also what hurt more is that when I was under so much mental strain, my husband did not stand by me. At that time I used to wish for a nuclear family, where you can be on your own and need not bother about others. I used to dream about being independent.

I feel bad about being illiterate. I am not confident because of that. My daughters are so different. They can talk to anyone and go anywhere they need to, by themselves. I realize that it is their education which was given them this confidence. I regret that I never had a chance to finish, at least, my S.S.L.C. (Secondary School Leaving Certificate).

My children have done well academically and have studied beyond the S.S.L.C. One of my daughters has even done a double M.A. Three of them are teachers. It is not only that I sent them to school, but they had an interest in education. I brought up my children just as I was brought up. I was a very obedient girl and never interacted with boys. My neighbours used me as a model for bringing up their own children. I like to think that my children are also like that. All of them married the person we chose for them. They went to school and came straight home. That is the case even now, when they are employed. I strongly feel that girls should be brought up like that.

My present worry is that my children should live long, have good health and be happy. Three of my sons are yet to get married. My daughter-in-law and my family are getting on well. They take special care of me, no doubt. All of them are employed. So, they do the outside work, and I do the cooking. The rest of the time, I watch TV. I don't remember any of my education any longer, just a few numbers. But truthfully, there is no need. Tell me, what is the point of literacy for a person who has not seen the world and has known nothing but cooking and running a house? Except sometimes when I am watching T.V., my illiteracy has not created any problems for me. I enjoy even the advertisements. The television is a big boon as far as I am concerned; the whole family sits together and watches.

My exposure to outside world is very limited. The furthest I have been in my life is up to the nearest town, three km away. Even after my marriage, when my husband travelled, he never took me with him.

I still manage the house. Now that my sons are all employed, they give me their salary, and I manage the household. My husband or my children never interfere. I keep an account of all the money they bring from Mysore. Even though I have only studied up to class five, I can still manage the household accounts. I enjoy doing household work and managing the home. Cooking is so easy now—you have machines for everything!

I am leading a happy life now. I am on good terms with my relatives; my children are all employed and settled. My only concern now is my children's well-being. I suffered the most immediately after getting married.

Geetha

My name is Geetha. I am thirty-three years old and married. I have two boys, 6 and 4 years old. My husband works as a journalist for a local daily. I live in Malappuram District. I have an elder brother and a younger sister. Both my parents are retired teachers. I live with my parents, my children and my husband. I work as a block coordinator of the CBNP (Community Based Nutritional Program).

My mother has two sisters. Her youngest sister was not so affluent, so, my mother and her elder sister gave their share of the land to the younger sister. The place where we live now, belongs to our father. My mother had the right to decide what to do with her share of the property. I don't think I would be allowed to do that today.

Father's *tarawad* is in Pattambi. He was very concerned about us children and our character formation. My father is a (communist) party worker, and very active in the teachers' movement. Often he came home late. When he left us at home in the evening, he left the responsibility of the house to me. So I had to take care of my little sister, and organize other household chores like overseeing the people coming to pluck coconuts, those who came to milk the cows, clean the cattle shed, etc. I had to supervise. It was a very heavy burden for me at a young age. I never got time to play. My brother never helped me; he just went to the playground with his friends.

Often when my father came home late he would bring two or three people with him for food. So we were always providing food for two or three extra people. Some nights my mother would be too tired and she would just go to sleep even before father came home. Then in the morning after the guests had left, my parents would fight with each other.

Father didn't drink, gamble or smoke so when they fought, my mother's main complaint was that he had no concern for her health. My mother had an accident when I was in class three and broke her elbow joint. For a long time she wasn't able to use her right hand at all and I used to help her. So from a very early age I wasn't able to go and play with my friends in the playground. I used to feel angry that I was stuck doing household work at home when my friends and even my brother, could play as long as they wanted.

I was born in the same house in which we live now. Since both my parents were working and there was nobody from either of the families to come and look after us, we had a maid to take care of us. I was sent to school when I was three. There was no *anganvadi* or *balvadi* (village nursery school) then, so I would go along with my father, because father's school was nearby and mother was working in a far-off school. There was an aunt, my father's brother's wife, who was staying nearby. They were of great help to us.

Father was very strict; so we all had to be punctual. I studied in the same school till the seventh standard. My sister also started going to school at the age of three years. Father was a mathematics teacher, so if we made mistakes in calculation, he would get angry and beat us. Since father was interested in building our character, we had to be very careful of how we said things. If we used a vulgar word, father would get very angry. So we did use bad language, but only when father was not at home.

Mostly Bindu, my sister, and Azad, my brother fought with each other. I normally had the role of the mediator. Father only intervened in our affairs to give his final judgment. Mother never used to have time. That was a permanent complaint when we were young. When all the other mothers had the time to tie their children's hair, see them off to school, our mother was not at home when we left for school in the morning or when we came back in the afternoon. We came back tired and had to make tea for ourselves. My brother used to prepare the tea till I was old enough to make it. After coming back from school, we had to unlock the house, keep our bags, wash our hands and legs, and make tea. The thought itself is painful. And there was never anything at home other than bread or bananas. When other children, whose mothers were housewives, told us how their mothers used to keep things ready when they came back from school, we realized what we missed.

On holidays my mother would prepare all kinds of snacks. But on other days we used to miss her a lot. I didn't like this business of mothers going to work. My image of my mother is always that of the busy mother who had no time. I think that our childhood was quite miserable.

I had lot of friends in school and the teachers were quite good. It was a mixed school and boys and girls used to sit and play together in the lower classes. My sister and I were given a lot of encouragement in the primary classes, probably because father was quite active in school affairs at that time.

From upper primary onwards, the seating arrangement changed. Boys were asked to sit in one row, and girls in another row. Though we were still allowed to play together and compete against each other in sports, we were no longer allowed to sit together in class.

I used to get high marks in Hindi. My father was my mathematics teacher, and even though I did well he wouldn't give us any extra marks. Today things are so different; teachers try and give their own children better marks. We also had a very good English teacher; I remember enjoying my English classes.

Girls and boys in my school were equal; there was no discrimination. We used to hit each other, compete against each other in sports and the science exhibitions, and both girls and boys had to sweep the floor and swab it with cow dung. Nobody questioned it. Today if students are asked to sweep the floor at school, their parents will immediately question the school authorities.

When we reached high school, the whole atmosphere changed. Boys were in one class and girls in another. There was a big distance between the teachers and the students. We were not allowed to question anything. There was no encouragement. Once we reached high school, we were not supposed to see or talk to boys. It was very difficult for both the boys and the girls to get used to this separation. Teachers were always watching us. No one could understand why we were being distanced from the boys all of a sudden and nobody explained it to us. All we knew was that we became conscious that we were girls and talking to boys was somehow bad.

During sports and youth festivals, men used to come with their make up groups, but our teachers never allowed them to touch us and do our make up. We did not understand why this was so at the time. Suddenly, within two or three months we had become untouchables, unseeables. The whole situation created a lot of tension in the sense that my own friends such as Damodaran and Raghavan were distanced from me in school. And yet when they came home, my parents didn't stop us girls from interacting with my brother's friends.

Now my sister is working in that same school. She says that the teachers are still the same. There is a generation of teachers that thinks that they are protecting the girls by not allowing them to interact with boys. There are some young teachers who want to change things and improve the interactions between girls and boys and encourage them to learn together. But the senior teachers just don't allow it.

I attained puberty when I was thirteen. It was during my vacation and I had to do a dance performance the day after. I was really worried that mother would not let me perform. But fortunately, my aunt, who was to accompany me to the venue of the performance, agreed to take care of me. I never really had any restrictions after puberty. My mother told me I had to be more careful about my behaviour because I was grown up now, but nothing more than that.

Once I started my pre-degree at the Holy Family College, I had to stop dancing because there was too much to study and I couldn't find enough time. The Holy Family College was a private institution and by its name, you can tell what kind of place it was. It was run by nuns who were extremely strict. We had to wear uniforms and my daily torture was something called the prayer room. My father was a leftist and so we had been brought up in a very secular manner. At home we never prayed or lit a lamp. My father taught us to be progressive. We were open to all religions but practiced none. In fact, we used to eat in our Muslim neighbour's house, whereas other Hindus would think it dirty. We were taught to be human beings, not Muslims, Christians or Hindus.

I remember there was a neighbour of ours who was interested in me. I didn't like him at all; I thought he was not a nice person. I tried my best to avoid him but he would go out of his way to meet me. I think there were some political problems between his father and mine and he tried to use the situation to spoil our family name. Once he sent me a 'love letter' which could have been seriously misunderstood by my family. My mother saw the letter and asked me whether I was meeting this boy. The question itself was shocking to me because I was always so honest and truthful with my parents. I denied it and my parents believed me so the matter ended there.

I realize now that this kind of thing happens very often and it is an easy way to harass a woman. It raises doubts about her morality and even her family. The same rules do not apply to men, the incident did not harm my neighbour in any way but, if I had a less understanding father, it could have harmed me severely. I was only twenty years old when it happened but it gave me a lot of tension.

My father was always very open with us and trusted all of his children completely. That is why when he asked me about my feelings about Hariharan, I was completely honest with him. Hari was one of my brother's friends, a journalist, and someone who was always welcome in our household. Because he spent a lot of time in our house, Hari and I became friends and slowly I developed feelings towards him. My father understood my feelings for Hari and agreed to our marriage. It was held in school, a very simply 'party' marriage. No feast, just a cup of tea, and no dowry.

I was very keen to continue to study after marriage and complete my M.A. I even prepared for the exam but could not appear for it because I was pregnant. Both of us wanted to postpone having children, but it was an accident and we could do nothing about it. Hari named our first child. And even though I didn't really like the name I went along with it. When our second child was born one and a half years later, I chose the name.

We fight with each other a lot. It makes me angry that he always goes out and never takes care of the children. Even when he is at home, he sits and reads, rather than helping with the children. I wish he would also take care of them a little so we could share this burden.

It worries me that the children are influenced a great deal by television and films. They watch too much violence. I am busy in the house so I get very little time to sit with them and so my husband could very well teach the children how to view such programmes and explain some values to them. This is the kind of problem that can only be solved if both parents are involved. If I tell my children that most of the violence they see on television is fake, they will never believe me. But if he explains it to them they will definitely believe him. Without our knowledge they have already imbibed the idea that their mother knows nothing.

If I try and explain all this to Hari, he gets angry. 'You should understand that I am a journalist and I am busy, I have responsibilities.' But I don't think that is good enough. Men have to find the time to involve themselves equally with their children. I think my siblings and I are better human beings today because our father involved himself in our upbringing.

I also worry about things like the idea of caste and religion. My siblings and I were brought up in a very secular way, we never thought about what a person's caste or religion was. Children nowadays, seem to be always talking about religion and caste. The other day I heard my son telling someone, 'Oh, he is a Muslim that is why he is dirty!' I scolded him and explained to him that anyone can be dirty, Hindus, Muslims, Christians, and showed him some examples. But he was not convinced and went to his father. My husband explained the same thing to him and suddenly my son believed everything.

I do not understand how this has happened in my household. I try and teach my children secular values and equality. Women's burdens are increasing every day. Apart from just cooking and cleaning for your children, one has to now, take care of their lessons and homework, monitor what they watch on TV, be careful of what values they imbibe, and make them good human beings who understand right and wrong. In a nuclear family, the woman's burden is greater because she has no help. So if one's husband shares the process of child-rearing then it becomes easier. Men need to understand that helping out does not just refer to helping in the kitchen.

The happiest moment in my life was when Hari and I decided to get married. We have been happily settled since our marriage till I faced a problem a few years ago. Hari became interested in another woman. She is a well-known intellectual. I had just had my second child and was suffering from post-natal depression. A number of people blamed the incident on me and said that I had not taken proper care of Hari and, therefore, obviously he would look elsewhere. I did not understand how I could have made him do this. It didn't make any sense. He was interested in another woman and yet everyone was blaming it on me. As always, my father came to my rescue. He suggested that I should talk openly with Hari and then depending on what Hari said, I should take a decision based on my conscience. My father told me that Hari could not help but love me and the best thing to do would be to discuss the situation. I agreed with my father and decided it was better to talk to Hari and listen to what he had to say.

What upset me was that even though I knew I had the confidence to manage the situation, people around us just blamed it on me. Before this incident, Hari always informed me where he was going and when he would be back. Our society allows him to go out and meet people freely, something that women are not allowed to do. If

I go astray it is my fault, if he goes astray, again is it my fault? Where is the sense in this?

I never continued my education after my first pregnancy. I still haven't done my post-graduation and am disappointed about that. Now we live with my parents and I am able to pursue my studies again. I have worked as a computer operator at the University of Calicut, a clerk in the publication department, and now with CBNP. Working at CBNP is interesting; I meet a lot of people and work with them on their problems personally. Though I enjoy my current job, I want to get a better job. I am studying for the Public Service Commission tests.

Right now, my work with CBNP is mostly fieldwork. These days Hari is on night duty and so we seldom see each other. He is home during the day and by the time I get back from work, he has left. But on Saturdays and Sundays, we spend a lot of time together. Our relationship has improved. We have more faith in each other and talk to each openly and frankly, and this openness has improved our understanding of each other.

The *tarawad* house is for me. We also have some more land. Financially we are quite safe and secure. My main aim in life at the moment, is to get a good job without having to give a donation. I am confident that I will find one.

Haseena

My parents had six children, two boys and four girls. I was the youngest. I have studied up to the fifth standard. I have been married twice and have a child. My husband works in the Gulf and comes to visit once a year. I was born in Chulliyode, Malappuram district. I lived with my parents till I was thirteen years old. We had a very good life as children.

We owned some property in Chulliyode, but my father lost all the property when he married off my sisters. With no property he felt ashamed to live in our village amongst friends and relatives, and so we shifted to Moothedath. We lived in Moothedath for nine years. It is here that I went to school and my childhood friends are all there.

The school was quite far from the house. A lot of boys and girls from our neighbourhood went to the same school, so we all used to walk together. There would be no gender differentiation. We would all play together, buy gooseberries together and even quarrel amongst ourselves. Around the time that I entered the third standard my mother told me that I was not supposed to mingle with boys so closely and that while going to school, the girls should go separately.

Madrasa education was a must for us. The madrasa only gave us religious teaching. While school education was secular, at the madrasa we were taught how to be good Muslim women. In some respects, a madrasa and school education are similar, but overall, they were entirely different.

After dinner my father would take me out with him for a walk; it would be just the two of us. Since I was the youngest, my father would take me everywhere with him. This helped me a lot. My sisters who weren't treated the same way are now scared to go out anywhere on their own. I don't feel scared; if I need to do some work I just go. My sisters need an escort even if they are going to see the doctor.

I reached puberty when I was thirteen years old. After puberty my parents became very restrictive about my movements and my behaviour. I was monitored and controlled all the time and both my parents would instruct me how I was to walk and talk in public. They made me aware and conscious of the fact that I had become a 'woman'. I didn't like it because before that I was friendly with some of the boys in the neighbourhood and then suddenly, I wasn't supposed to talk to them at all. I still wanted to play and go to school, but my parents stopped my schooling and I wasn't allowed to go to the playground.

I don't remember anything about my first marriage. I just remember that I did not like it. I was very young and knew nothing at the time. My husband's approach to me, to sex, the atmosphere in his house, everything was negative. I stayed there for only a few days and then came home.

I came back from my first marriage and moved back in with my parents. But things were difficult financially and I felt that I should contribute something to the running of the house. I decided to learn a skill. I started taking tailoring classes. A friend of my father's, a Nair by caste, lived nearby. His son ran a tailoring shop and it was he who taught me most of what I learnt about tailoring.

Of course, his caste and religion became a big problem for everyone in the neighbourhood. People began to spread rumours about us. I just wanted to earn a living to help my parents and people assumed that I was doing something immoral. I think everyone expected me to be a quiet, religious girl who didn't leave the house, but that was impossible. Since I have learnt tailoring I now have an income and am getting many orders. The boy who taught me was like a brother to me, we are still friends. In fact, it was he who arranged my second marriage.

My second marriage occurred much later, when I was twenty-three. By then I was earning a decent income and was more mature. I was initially against a second marriage. But my relatives and friends said that it was important to get married and have a family so that someone would always take care of me. I thought they were right and agreed to a second marriage.

My second husband already had a wife and three children when we got married. I never asked him why he decided to take a second wife. To other people he said, 'I am capable of taking care of two women and two families. Some time back, I didn't have the money to buy a single beedi, but now I can take care of two families.' My parents enquired about his and collected whatever details were required. They were satisfied with him. I knew that they were worried about their financial situation. Who else would come forward and want to marry me, especially when they could not give any dowry.

My parents couldn't afford to give me a dowry for both my marriages. The boy's side gave me *mehr* and took me in marriage. I am against the dowry system; it causes too much suffering to the parents. I will refuse to accept dowry money when my children get married.

I have one son. I have not had a PPS as yet. I conceived with great difficulty and doctors told me I should not conceive again for at least, five years. But one year later, my husband came from the Gulf and I was pregnant. After six weeks I was bleeding too much and the doctors told me to have an abortion. After that we decided not to have any more children. As long as my husband is working in the Gulf, we can afford a good education for our son. He is going to a convent school. My husband also thinks that education is important.

I am a tailor, but after my cesarean, I was not able to sew, because I have a very bad back. But I am still interested in working. Both men and women should work to share the burden in the family.

Often I feel I made a mistake marrying my husband. He and his first wife are on very good terms. Unnecessarily I entered the happily married life of another woman. If my father had been able to pay a proper dowry then I could have easily had a different marriage. I feel isolated, because it is obvious that they love each other very much. On the other hand, I feel that he loves me as well, and takes care of my son and me. He gives us regular money for maintenance. With his money, my family, that is, my sister's family, my brother's children, and me, all live comfortably.

I am not interested in politics; I am not a Party member and I don't know anything about political movements. Some years ago I read a book on Soviet Russia, but I felt that I could not understand it properly, and stopped reading.

My parents are the most important people in my life. When this second marriage proposal came I only agreed because it made my parents happy. I would have preferred not to have to leave my natal home. In fact I even told my husband that I would only marry him if he allowed me to live with my parents. When my father died, I was in shock. Then when my mother died a month later, I found it very difficult to go on with my life. I still find it very difficult in their absence. My parents' death is the only sorrow in my life.

Two of my sisters have left their children with me. My brother also spends a lot of time with us. I see my husband often when he is here from the Gulf. Both of us live happily and never fight. I have adjusted to my sister-in-law and mother-in-law who come and go from my house sometimes. I am content. I would be happy if my life would continue just like this. I am not ambitious; I simply don't want my child to starve.

Pushpa

I was born when we were living with my father's family as a joint household. I am twenty-eight years old. I was very good at school but my situation was such that after the seventh standard I was forced to stop. My father was an alcoholic. My mother worked and earned enough to raise us, what my father earned was not even enough to buy his alcohol.

I have an older brother, then myself; after me, my sister and my younger brother. Even when I was going to school I used to do all the housework for them and then leave. I stopped studying for the sake of my younger siblings, so I could take care of them.

We owned fifty cents of land. When it was divided my father got his *tarawad*. I was born there. My mother used to do all the farm work. She also had a steady job at the place where my father worked. In those days wages were extremely low, but the prices of commodities were also equally low so my mother's small income could sustain our household.

Once I stopped going to school I also started working. My elder brother started working in the workshop for about Rs 70 per week, after he finished middle-school. With our additional incomes it became easier to meet household expenses.

When I was in school, there was one teacher who took a special interest in me and helped me with my work. She was related to the people for whom my father worked and understood my home situation. She also helped me by buying me clothes and books. Up to the fifth standard I was studying in a co-educational school, and then from the sixth onwards, boys and girls were separated.

I wanted to study further, but after the seventh standard I would have had to enroll in the Ollari Convent, which was very expensive. We could not even afford the uniforms and it would have adversely affected my younger siblings' education. So I stopped studying to further their education. Besides the eighth standard requires much more work and with all the housework I was doing, I didn't have time for it.

I was twelve when I attained puberty. My parents conducted a large ceremony at home and invited more than 150 people for the feast. Puberty was the real reason why I stopped going to school. The ceremony occurred during my exams. Generally people believed that once a girl reached puberty she was not to go to school and was supposed to stay home and take over household responsibilities.

Once my mother left for work at 7.00 a.m., I was responsible for my elder brother and younger siblings. As the eldest daughter, it was my duty. I would cook their food, bathe the younger ones, and get them ready for school. In all of that I had no time for myself.

My younger sister did not really want to study and stopped after the sixth standard. My younger brother completed up to eighth standard and even appeared for his pre-degree exams. But he developed a problem with his legs and stopped studying. He now works in a goldsmith's shop.

Till I was eighteen I worked on Josettan's land and in his house. It was a nice environment to work in. Then I got married when I was nineteen. My husband was my neighbour. We have two sons, the older is eight years old and the younger one, two-and-a-half. My husband loves me very much; he works hard and doesn't drink or smoke too much. Our wedding took place in a grand manner; more than five hundred people were invited. His family asked for Rs 3,000 and three gold sovereigns as dowry, but we could not afford that. They never complained.

I have started working again to help my husband. We have a good life, when you come to think of it. When you compare us to others we are relatively well off. I think that if you work hard, you can live well. If you are lazy, that won't be the case. We are able to look after our needs well; we can even send the children for tuition and hire autos to take them. Because both of us are working, we can do all of this.

My husband is a union worker and a wage labourer. The union he is in, doesn't make much money. In some areas, unions make good money. He is basically a head load worker. When he is called to till land, he does that as well. What he earns in a week in the union, he can earn in two days from working as a wage labourer. That is why we accept work on the land.

His family was against our marriage. They were, and are our immediate neighbours. They knew about my father's drinking and because of that, they opposed the match. For the first year and a half, we lived as a joint family in his parent's house. When his mother fell ill, his father and elder brother accused me of being an ill omen that had brought illness to their house. My husband fell out with his father because of this. That was when we started staying in my house, next door to them. For two years we lived in my house, and then for another two years, we lived in a rented house. During this time my husband's house was partitioned and we received Rs 18,000 as our share. We used that money to buy two-and-a-half cents of land. Recently we have built a pukka house.

When we first got married I used to be paid Rs 9 per day. Now things have changed so much, my wage is Rs 60 per day. I also go for outside work now. One has to, our expenses have risen and so we need the money.

I had been married for two years when my first son was born. I was very worried, because it had taken me so long to conceive. Then six years later, my second son was born and we were happy. My husband would have liked a daughter. He is very fond of girls. In fact he would have been very happy if even our first-born had been a daughter. If my second-born had been a daughter then I would have had a tubectomy, but now he says he will only allow me to have an operation after we have a daughter. I don't think he can visualize or understand the financial difficulties we might have to face if we continue to have children.

My mother takes care of my sons. She is no longer physically capable of working so I leave my sons with her when I go to work. She sends my elder son to school and looks after the younger one during the day.

My father used to beat up my mother very badly. My elder brother used to be too scared to stand up to our father; if he stood up to father, he would get beaten as well. I would wail and cry loudly and the neighbours would come and help. My husband's family were our neighbours and in those days, helped us a great deal. They would come running and pull my parents apart. They would give us children shelter for the night till my father had gone to sleep. They were very good to us. I have undertaken many fasts and vows at churches and temples and prayed for my father to get better. But to no avail, he told me 'I began drinking at twelve, it will take me. I will drink till I die. I have no choice.'

My father still drinks, but he does not get violent any more, he has become quiet. My brother is now a bigger drunkard than my father ever was. He is only thirty-two, but he gets drunk and is more violent than my father used to be. How can my mother ever have any peace of mind?

Every morning I wake up at 4.00 a.m., and have everything ready by 8.00 a.m. I get the children ready and leave them with my mother. My husband's work is very close to our house, so he is always at hand if there is an emergency. In the evening, there is always some work in the house and I look after that. My husband helps in the kitchen. I had to explain to him that an individual cannot work outside and also within the home; that I need help. So he does things for me. I told him, 'I will not work if you don't help me in the house and then how will we manage without my additional income?' At first he didn't know how to do anything, but now he can do it all—peel onions, cut vegetables. Sometimes when he has no work he will even do the sweeping and mopping, and cook rice and curry before I come home.

It is important that he helps me since none of our relatives are particularly helpful. We do not bear ill will towards anyone; it is just the way things are. We do not have the time to get into arguments with our neighbours. Now we even visit my sister-in-law's house, but at the time of our marriage we were not on good terms. Now relationships are more cordial and that makes me happy.

My husband and I eat our meals together. When I was a child my father would give me a small portion of his meal, now my husband gives me a portion of his meal. Even after I have served him, my husband takes a small handful of rice and keeps it aside on his plate for me. Only once I have that, is my stomach full.

I worry about the future. I worry about my husband; he is overweight and I worry about his health. Near our house there is a man with three children, the oldest, only sixteen years old. His wife has a mental illness; she doused herself in kerosene and set herself on fire. She was burnt badly, but survived. The man himself is a wage labourer and also works as a tree-cutter, but he does not keep well. I look at that family and wonder, 'who do those children have?' That is what scares me. I have no support from my own family, my father and brother are both drunkards. And how can I assume support will come from my husband's family? Until recently we were estranged, I feel sometimes that we have nobody.

Financially, we are all right. We have a small chit-fund,but my husband does not save very much money. What I earn, I hand over to him. He looks after all the household expenses. When I need something for the house, I tell him and he buys it.

I have a problem with my left knee. If I am squatting in the bathroom, and have to rise, I need to wait a minute before stretching my left leg. That apart, I am fine, without any major illness. In the past, I used to get headaches. Now that has ceased.

Ever since I was a child I always went to both temples and churches. When I worked with Josettan, I was influenced by their connection with the church. When something was weighing on my mind I would go into their prayer room and get down on my knees and pray. Most of my prayers were answered and this reinforced my faith in the church. That does not mean I am not a Hindu any longer, or that I want to convert. I am insistent that I should be allowed to profess my faith the way that I want to. I don't like it when people come and try and preach to me, and I have the same policy with others. Everyone is welcome to his own particular belief and way of worshipping.

I am quite happy with my life, but they say that every happiness brings with it some kind of sorrow. When I am sad or confused or worried, I go down on my knees and pray.

Sudhakumari

I am forty-three years old. My *illam* (a *Namboodiri* joint family household) is in Kottarakkara and my husband's is in Kottayam. I live in Calicut with my husband and two daughters. My elder daughter is doing her Masters in Computer Application (M.C.A) while the younger one has recently finished her S.S.L.C exams and is applying for further studies. I did my postgraduate degree in Malayalam after I was married. More recently I have completed my L.L.B (law degree). I do not practice, however. I am a housewife. My husband is a professor of Sanskrit. My father-in-law died many years, but my husband's mother is still alive. He has two sisters and three brothers.

In my family my parents had five children, of whom I am the eldest. I have three younger sisters and a brother. Both my parents are still alive. We lived in a large joint family, with my paternal grandparents and great-grandmother and all my uncles and cousins. My great grandmother died twenty years ago; she was an extremely independent woman, even though she was illiterate. My great-grandfather was a progressive man, whose family was ostracized from the community.

My great-grandmother, my father's maternal grandmother, had only one daughter; that is my father's mother. Since they had no sons, my great-grandmother got her husband to marry again. She conducted his second marriage herself, but they still had no sons. Finally, she adopted a boy from another *illam* as her own son. When great-grandfather died, the adopted boy wanted all the property. During the partition, the second wife took all the land, which was debt-free.

My great-grandmother got the area with *pattakadam* (land with debt). Everyone exploited her, and still my great-grandmother struggled and survived. At that time, none of our own relatives, or people from our community helped her. Instead, other caste members, like a Muslim, who was a diamond merchant and was the *kudiyan* (tenant) of our ancestral land assisted her.

My great-grandmother was widowed at the age of twenty-three and my grandmother was widowed at the age of twenty-six. My grandmother was treated very badly in her in-laws' house. She was made to work and not given proper food. She had to fight to survive in that house. One day my great-grandmother saw how bad the treatment had become and brought her daughter and my father back home, to live with her.

I had a very interesting childhood. I believe that my generation enjoyed their childhood far more than the previous or the present generations. The present generation lives in a nuclear set up and so, things have become more individualized. The previous generation was not given the freedom and opportunities that my generation had. Things that were denied to my mother, such as an education, were available to me. My childhood was a good mixture of tradition and modernity.

My mother used to question the son preference that everyone had at that time. She used to say, 'Why a preference for sons? We don't get our girls from the gutter! Women exert the same amount of labour pain for girls as they do for boys, so how can girls be inferior?' But still, I believe that my brother was given extra care because he was the only boy. It was not that he was given better food, or taken to better doctors; it just felt that my great-grandmother, grandmother and mother were very particular about my brother; that no evil eye should fall on him, that he should not get injured.

When we were young, there were some financial difficulties. This is not to say that we were not given enough food to eat or our education suffered. But we didn't get new dresses very often. In Kerala most households buy new clothes during Onam and Vishu festivals but we only got new clothes at Onam. At home, we wore a *mundu* (dhoti) but when we went out, we wore a *pavada* (full skirt).

My father finished his studies after he was married. I was in the seventh standard when he finished his degree. I remember there was no transport for him to go to college, the only vehicle was a *karivandi*, a bus run on coal. Because of the transport problem, my father stopped his education. It was a pity, because he was very interested in the fine arts, and drama. He used to work in the field with the other labourers.

My mother was the eldest child in her family, which was very traditional. Since my father's family was extremely progressive, marrying my father was quite difficult for my mother.

When we were children we were assigned different household tasks in the morning, such as sweeping. To avoid fights we used to share all the work. Only my brother was exempt from these chores. Then we would apply oil to our heads and go to our pond. Our house was an *ettukettu* (house with eighteen rooms). I would take all the children and wash all their clothes. Once my sisters were old enough to wash their own clothes then everyone washed their clothes themselves. But since we had only one brother, I washed his clothes for him even once he was grown up. We used to enjoy ourselves at the pond. All of us had been taught to swim when we were three years old, so we used to play in the water. We used to play hide and seek and catch and run in the water.

In other households, games would be different for boys and girls. We would make *ola* balls (balls made out of coconut leaves) and play just like the boys. But other girls never came out; they sat inside and played *pallankuzhi,* an indoor game. We were lucky; we had no restrictions and used to roam around the entire *parambu* (open space surrounding a homestead).

Being the oldest I had more responsibilities than my siblings. I was expected to take care of the younger children and especially watch out for my brother. Also it was my duty to look after Unni (my great-grandmother). But none of this affected my studies. I had a systematic routine so it was very easy.

My brother was more involved with work outside the house than we were. When someone came to visit, my grandmother would call him and discuss things in his presence. On the other hand, the girls were not supposed to show themselves at all when someone came to visit. All the shopping was his job, though we were allowed to accompany him.

My grandmother loved listening to stories. We would all sit up late at night with her while my father read stories aloud to her. Horror stories were forbidden, since then, we might get scared. In the evenings, we would finish our homework, do *namam chollal* (say our prayers), recite our multiplication tables, eat dinner and then sit down with grandmother while father told us a story.

Our father was extremely hot-tempered. He was also very interested in literature and was always reading or writing something. Whenever we did something wrong, we would keep very quiet, or else father would beat us.

Our school was near the house, so we were able to come home for lunch. It was a Malayalam-medium school. Because we were of a higher caste than everyone else, we were never punished or beaten in school. But when we got into trouble the master would come home and complain to our father who then punished us.

Our school was co-educational; girls sat on one side of the classroom and boys on the other. The biggest punishment you could get was to be made to sit on the opposite side of the classroom that is for a girl to be made to sit on the boys' side or vice versa. We were all scared of that punishment! After lower primary, I studied in a management school because the government school was too far away. When we came back from school we would have to wash our hands and legs properly before entering the house.

My parents had a very peaceful relationship. Even after my father got married, my grandmother was the head of the household and used to guide him in most matters. But my father would not take a decision at home without consulting my mother first. He would ask her opinion and she would always say, 'You decide, there is no need for me to tell you my opinion. I want only what you want.' My father, however, used to insist that my mother told him what she wanted. I still remember my mother had come from such an orthodox family so she was an introvert and timid in front of everyone. It was just the way she was brought up.

When I was in class five, my father joined the F.L. (law) course in Trivandrum. So the family shifted to Trivandrum. My grandmother wanted to buy a house in Trivandrum for all of us, but we could not afford it, so we rented a house instead. My sister and I, the older children, went with my parents, while my younger siblings stayed with my grandmother. It was only a few kilometres away from our house but I still felt very sad when we were parted.

Some years later we bought a house in Trivandrum, which is where my parents still live. I first went to a lower primary school and then shifted to Model School. My sister was in school with me, but she then fell ill with jaundice and my grandmother insisted that my sister go home with her. So after that I was all alone.

When I was in the sixth standard, I had my first period. My mother saw it first and she started crying. I was only 11 years at the time and

in nuclear families, children insist on their independence and realize their individuality. Also it is convenient to live in joint family; if we had to go somewhere there would never be any question about leaving the children. There are always enough people to help look after them. There are other issues as well, for instance, last week Master had to attend a workshop at Kalady University and therefore the children and I were alone. There was a phone call at 11.00 p.m. telling me that my mother-in-law was ill, but I could not go and see her because there was nowhere to leave my daughters and I could not take them with me at that time of the night. If I were in a joint family I would have never had this kind of problem.

When I first got married, my father told me, 'There are a lot of members in that household, and all of them come from different homes, they have different tastes and interests and you will have to adjust to their moods. Don't ever complain about them or give them any chance to complain about you. Whatever happens, bear it and you always know that whenever you need my help I will be with you.'

I conceived a year and a half after I was married. We wanted to have our children early because Master felt that our age difference was substantial, he was eleven years older. Initially, we had a lot of financial problems, my husband's younger brother was still studying, his sister's marriage had just been completed and his father's income was quite small. My elder brother-in-law was unemployed with two children.

We had a total of twelve and a half acres of land. When this land was divided my father-in-law gave more to *aphan*, his brother, since he had more daughters. I began to see a difference between the natal home and the marital home. But I always remembered my father's words; I never complained. When I was pregnant, my father-in-law had a fall and had to undergo two operations at a private hospital. I was anxious at the time because I had a complication—an Rh Factor problem with my baby, but I decided not to mention it to even my husband.

My first delivery was normal, but then after two years, I had a miscarriage. Since I had an Rh Factor problem I needed to be doubly careful. And so we waited six years before I conceived again. Thankfully my second delivery was also normal. After my second daughter I had an operation. My mother-in-law was upset that I had an operation without trying for a son, but she came around to my decision, and now loves her granddaughters.

I did not really want to work. There was no pressure from either side for me to work. My husband was insistent that whatever I decided

I should not be idle, so I studied further and completed my post-graduate and L.L.B course.

We have tried our best to bring up our children in a secular atmosphere. I have not told them tradition is meaningless, but try and encourage them to think about the scientific meanings behind the rituals. Even when my daughters reached puberty, I did not have any ceremony for them, instead I gave them proper information about what was happening to their bodies and what to expect.

We built a small house for ourselves at Vazhoor. We were keen to build a house near my husband's parents. It is a small two-bedroom house of medium size. Soon after the construction work started my brother-in-law met with an accident. The people in that area are highly superstitious and refused to continue working until he was cured. Then soon after we finished the house, my husband's sister became very ill and was admitted to hospital. My sister-in-law died and after that it was very difficult to get anyone to work on the house. My husband was busy with work and so I decided to go there and arrange things. It was very difficult. Going on my own to the cement shop, timber market and bargaining with the traders. People found it very difficult to adjust to a woman doing these things. I would constantly hear people say 'Look the *antharjanam* (Namboodiri woman—a derogative term) is here again!' Finally I had to say to them, 'My family has no problem with what I am doing and nor do I, so then what is your problem? Also when it is necessary, even *antharjanams* may do anything which men can do.' What is interesting is that, both men and women gossiped about me. This, I suppose, is the peculiarity of Kerala, women are as bad as men with regard to these things. Though there is not much open discrimination, there is a sharp distinction between the roles of men and women. Certain jobs are designated as men's jobs and women are not supposed to do them. And if women chose to or had to do those jobs, they were subject to mockery and abuse.

The criticism bothered me. There I was, working hard everyday, building my confidence and the local people just belittled me and made life difficult for me because I was a woman. What was funny was that later, these same people came and asked me for help and advice when they were building their own houses My grandmother encouraged me; she always used to say that as women we needed to have a backbone that never bends and a tongue that never tires (*valayatha navum thalaratha nattellum*).

I only get a chance to glance at the headlines in the morning; I read the newspaper in detail only in the afternoon once all my work is over. The busiest time for an employed or unemployed woman is always the morning. Other kinds of media, like the television and radio are good but one must be sensible about them. The TV has a number of channels, which are both informative and entertaining, but children seem to get caught up in only the entertainment. This has a strong influence on their culture. Children today seem to spend all their time in front of a TV; as a consequence they are getting a different picture of life, gender relations and human relations. It is not real life; but still children seem to accept these values.

I believe I am a social being, a confident person who has her own way of doing things. If someone says that I am wrong, I am always ready to rethink and change my path.

Vasanthi

My name is Vasanthi, I am thirty-eight years old. I gave my S.S.L.C exams but failed. I was born and studied in Trivandrum. From the fifth standard onwards I also worked as a domestic maid; I studied and worked through school. My elder sisters and brother did not study very far. I was the only one who studied till the tenth, even while working as a housemaid.

My father used to drink. He was working with a public address system when he got an electric shock. After that he left that job. He was very fond of us and loved my mother. He never beat us, even when he was drunk.

One of my employers looked after me as if I were their own child. They encouraged me to go to school, even though I was weak in studies. I worked in three houses at that time, and was always late for school. Everyday the teacher would scold me. I stopped studying after I failed the S.S.L.C. exams.

Even though we were poor I was married to an employed man. I was working till the day before my marriage. Now I have two daughters. The older one is ten-and-a-half years old and the younger one, nine. They are both studying in a Malayalam medium school. They are very bright.

My brother was the only boy in our family and therefore, my mother used to favour him with more food and better clothes. My sisters and I had to do the housework before going to school and then work in other houses afterwards, but my brother did nothing. My mother still takes more interest in his life than she does in ours.

I was always given the money to buy our food supplies. After school I would go to a nearby evening market and buy rice, fish, tapioca, tamarind, chillies and anything else we needed. We never ate anything all day. In the morning we would eat the leftovers from the previous day's meal. In classes one to five we were given an afternoon meal in the school, but after sixth standard, there were no afternoon meals.

I attained my puberty at thirteen. My parents informed everyone in the neighbourhood and I was made to sit on a plank in front of everyone. Even though we were poor we had a ceremony. After that, I was not allowed to come out of the house, go to the temple or see any males. This restriction on seeing males only happened the first time we had our period. Since then I haven't had very many restrictions. I have to wear full skirts now and not go out by myself in the evenings. But that is all.

When my elder sisters got married the marriage expenses had to be borne out of all of our earnings. My father was ill and it was difficult for him to earn the money for our marriages. My brother started working only when he was seventeen, so for a long time, my earnings were very important in the family. Since I was working and studying there was no rest for me. It was a very tough time, but my work paid off and I made enough money to give eight sovereigns of gold and Rs 10,000 as my own dowry. It was an arranged marriage. He was from the same caste as I am, the *Janaka Samudayam* (*jolsyam* caste). Then the owners of the house in which I used to work met the expenses of my wedding. So my marriage was much easier for my parents.

My husband had a job in the Railways. If I had known that he was an alcoholic, I would have never married him. Not only was he an alcoholic but also he harassed me regularly. I found out later that the doctor had said he had a mental illness which had started when he was eighteen years old. It was a hereditary disorder.

When we got married my husband was working in Maharashtra, but he had quit that job because of his mental instability. I did not know this at the time. Once I intercepted a letter from his sister enquiring about his illness and that is how I came to know about his mental problems. At that time I desperately wanted to come back to my natal home. My husband had treatment but he never returned to work. Early in our marriage, my husband would switch from caring about me to beating me or harassing me very quickly. He never gave me any money and I would have to cook food with whatever he would bring or I could find. He always found fault with my cooking.

Then when I was carrying my first child he said that the child was not his. I conceived two months after our marriage. I would go to the railway hospital for check ups but I was weak. During my seventh month I went to my natal home. Throughout my pregnancy he used to come home drunk. I had enough to eat when I was pregnant but I never had a moment of peace of mind.

Sometimes we would go and watch Hindi movies together. If by accident, I glanced at another man, the day would be spoilt. If I looked out of the house, he would ask me who I was looking at. Most of the time he kept the door locked.

Since he never allowed me to go out, I had no contact with my neighbours. Also it was a different place so I did not speak the language or know my way around. I could have learnt if he had just let me interact with other people,but he did not like that.

I had a good physique and good health before I was married. After marriage I became weak and contracted some kind of skin disease. My husband told me I had leprosy and wanted to throw me out of the house. He never let me go for treatment and even now though my skin is okay, I have scars all over my body.

I was scared to say anything to him because I knew that if he didn't like what I said he would beat me up. Whenever he asked me something I answered with fear. He didn't work, or look after the children. I was depressed. But even then I wish that wherever he is, he should be all right.

My husband's only good quality was that he never had an extra-marital relationship. Even though we parted over two years ago, I still trust him. It is wrong for a man to have an extra-marital relationship, whether you are happy or not you have to live with the person you are married to. If a person goes off to someone else it is not healthy.

Six months after I had my first child I went back to my husband's house because I did not want to be a burden on my parents. No matter how bad a man he was, he was still my child's father. After seeing the child, my husband changed for a little while and became kind. But that did not last very long, and soon he was back to his old ways again.

After I went back to my husband's house, he was not working because he was mentally ill. He would start a job and then quit after a few days saying he could not do it because of his illness. This carried on for some time and after two months I left again and went back to my parents. There was no way for me to survive there. At least if I was to be at my parent's house I could go out and work and bring up my children properly.

Soon after I returned to my parent's house I realized that I was expecting again. My second daughter is one and a half years younger than my first. My husband came to be with me when I delivered our second child. My mother had to take care of the delivery expenses because we had no money. After my second child I had a hysterectomy and then once I was well again I started looking for a job in a house nearby. My mother helped me by looking after the child. My husband was unhappy that I had a hysterectomy, but we had no choice, we could barely feed our two children what was the point in having a big family.

I work in four houses, earn a total of Rs 2,100 per month and can now afford to buy milk for my children.

Now my father, mother, my two children and I stay together in a house and next door is my brother, his wife and their two children. Finally, I feel safe again. I live separately from my husband. It is a good thing.

I have never faced any kind of sexual harassment in my twenty five years of working in these households. Except once before I was married in a house where there was a boy who was younger than I was, I sensed his behaviour change towards me. I told his mother, who was a teacher, about the boy's behaviour. She spoke to her son and made him understand that I was like his sister and he should behave properly towards me. Since then he has been fine.

I was a disciplined girl when I was young. I never mingled with men excessively. Now I am freer. It's not that talking to men is wrong; but it is very easy to get a bad name. If I talk to one or two men on my way to work, there are five others who are watching and say 'look she talks to all the men on the road.' People never see the good in you, only the bad. Our whole society is like that. I am lucky that from the first time I went to work, people have only had a good opinion about me and my behaviour.

Even though we are poor, I always give food to any beggar who comes to my house. This ensures that my children will always have food as well. I have to buy each and everything I require for the house. The houses where I work often give me a few things, like food or clothes, which is a help, but I still have to take care of the children. My mother helps me by doing all the household work.

When I was married to my husband, there was no freedom for me to take part in decision-making. But now I take all the decisions with regard to my household, my children and myself. He didn't even give me the freedom to visit my neighbours. Now I am free without him. If I want to go somewhere I go, if I want to work I work.

I still have to struggle a lot because I have to take care of five people. If my father falls sick, it is my responsibility. My mother has high blood pressure and uterus problems. Now my elder daughter helps me with the household work. My brother next door got an electricity connection, which we share, but that means I have to pay half the bill for that. Also we took a loan to build the houses. The loan is in my name and so I am responsible for paying the instalment every month.

I am scared that my children only have me. If I were to fall ill what would happen to them? I have high blood pressure. Also I am prone to depression and sadness. I don't have the happiness of having a family and a husband who works and looks after the children and me. It worries me.

I am sad that we could not live as a family. However, I control my feelings. I want to live. I do not want to die. Why should people die just because things do not work?

I work hard so I can have the things I want in my life.

Gender Disparity in Kerala: Some Visual Images

This section consists of some photographs of women from contemporary Kerala. It visually complement the arguments in the book. They have been taken from different parts of the state in the year 2006, and cover women from different social backgrounds.

The pictures reveal the fact that activities of women in Kerala are by no means restricted to the private sphere, nor do the women cover their heads and bodies in the manner women may do in some other parts of the country. Women in Kerala share the public space with men in a variety of ways. They queue up for, and travel in, public transport (1 and 2), exercise their electoral rights (3), take part in protests and demonstrations (4, 9, and 10), and perform religious ceremonies (6).

However, a closer look at the photographs brings out the very structured nature of this sharing. It reveals a kind of 'gendered' conduct not quite expected in a society where both men and women have been exposed to such high levels of education. In each of these pictures, women and men operate within spatially defined boundaries, occupying spaces clearly demarcated for each sex. This is evident from not just from the manner in which men and women take part in special religious ceremonies, but also from the separate queues, rows, and seats reserved for women in public transport: a space that is shared by both the sexes in their everyday lives. It is interesting to note that even during public demonstrations that involve forming of 'human chains' as a part of registering protest, protesters from the opposite sexes scrupulously desist from holding hands. The unspoken rules of gendered conduct take clear precedence over the chosen form of demonstration of worker solidarity for a 'cause' (4).

Some of the photographs in this section also bring out in sharp focus how women are divided by class and culture. Restrictions relating to gender relations are more severe for women from the middle and upper classes. This is evident from the body languages of poor women who sell fish and women from the more affluent classes who buy them (11); between the unfettered anger of activist fish vendors involved in a public protest (9) and the genteel and socially proper machinations of middle class service women participating in a demonstration (10).

A few pictures included in this section demonstrate the traditional as well as the newly evolving roles of women in Kerala. The Nangyaar Koothu performance (13) is a traditional dance form of Kerala in which participants are only women. Young women in photograph 12 are seen performing a traditional role albeit in the modern setting of a public function attended by political dignitaries.

Photograph 14 of a young woman pole-vaulter demonstrates that new kinds of career options such as in sports, are indeed opening up for women in Kerala. However, there is another side to these seemingly new openings. Sports in Kerala is an increasingly glamorized profession, and feminine glamour in some of its new avatars has public approval. Besides, after a sports career these women get absorbed into jobs that have a wide social acceptance.

The editor is grateful to Jipson Sikhera, photo journalist stationed in Cochin for the photographs, and J. Devika of the Centre for Development Studies, Thiruvanathapuram for providing overall supervision for the pictures contained in this section.

Editor

1. *The interior of a public bus*
The interior of a Kerala State Road Transport Corporation (KSRTC) city service bus. Here men and women travel together but are confined to strictly demarcated spaces allotted to them inside the bus.

2. *Men and women at the bus-stop*
Spatial separation of men and women in a bus-stop in the capital city of the state.

3. *Voters*

Voters in a polling booth, with two different queues for men and women.

4. *A human chain*

Photograph of a 'human chain' in a protest organized by a service organization in Thiruvananthapuram. Note how the chain gets broken when men and women happen to stand next to one another. The political imperatives of worker solidarity fail to transcend the socially ordained barriers of gender.

5. *Women and men in a temple*
Worshipping in a temple. Women and men are separated in different rows.

6. *Gender division during sacrificial rites*
Women offering sacrificial rites for ancestors on the banks of the Periyar at Aluva during the annual Karakadaka Vaavu festival. The photograph shows that although men and women are involved in a common ritual, they are still spatially separated from one another.

7. *Women and labour*
Early morning scene of tea plantation workers in Munnar. This kind of low paid work is done predominantly by women.

8. *Women agricultural labourers*
Women agricultural labourers carrying head loads and food for the day. Another low-paid work domain open to women workers from poor households.

9. *Fish vendors*
A demonstration by fish-vendors. The body language of the protestors is in striking contrast to that of the middle-class women protestors from a service organization seen in photograph 10.

10. *Middle-class women workers*
Protest by middle class women workers from some service organizations. This is how 'respectable women' should protest.

11. *Two women in a fish market*
Scene from a fish market. The photograph shows the different attitudes of the two women; one who is selling the fish and the other who is buying it, freezing as it were, the cultural distance between the two.

12. *Women in a 'decorative' role*

A group of young women holding the *taalappoli* in a public function in the capital city, which was attended by political dignitaries of the state. Serving such 'decorative' purposes in public functions is reserved only for women.

13. *Traditional women performers*

A Nangyaar Koothu performance. This is a form of drama in Sanskrit, and is unique to Kerala. This is traditionally performed only by women.

14. *Women in sports*
A woman pole-vaulter. With legends like P. T. Usha as inspiration, young women of Kerala have been entering the arena of sports in increasingly large numbers. It has acquired the legitimacy of a socially accepted profession and promises entry into 'respectable' jobs for women.

Index